Quick & Easy Cookbook

Published by Covenant Communications, Inc.
American Fork, Utah

Printed in China
First Printing: March 2013

20 19 18 17 16 15 14 13 3 10 9 8 7 6 5 4 3 2 1

ISBN-13 978-1-62108-343-6

MORMON PANTRY

Quick & Easy Cookbook

Delicious Meals in Minutes from the Bestselling Author of "Cooking for Two"

Debbie G. Harman

Table of Contents

Dost thou love life, then do not squander time, for that's the stuff life is made of.

Benjamin Franklin

Quick & Easy
Dinner Recipes

Originally built in 1886, the old pioneer home in which I live has a porch that spans the entire length of the house. It's a big, wonderful porch . . . that I never use. I am too busy!

I realized one day that my life is very different from those of the pioneers who built and lived in my home more than a hundred years ago. One of those differences is in how I make dinner. A meal that would have taken many hours for them to prepare can be made today in thirty minutes or less. Why?

Convenience. I think that word has changed our lives more than any other word in the English language. Electricity, manufacturing, automobiles, technology, and communication are just some of the many things that make our lives so convenient.

And as much as I love my old pioneer home, I am so grateful that I don't live in that time, because I understand that all these conveniences have given me just that: **TIME.**

Cooking with Convenience Foods

A few years ago I was surprised to find that in order to save time, many of my friends use packaged hash browns to make funeral potatoes. What a clever idea! I had never thought of doing that.

I realized that although I like the idea of quick and easy, I had never really been one to cook with convenience foods because many packaged foods are more expensive. But I learned that sometimes it's worth a few more pennies to save **TIME**.

Each time you prepare a meal, you must decide whether to use the convenient prepared items in your local grocery store that cost a little more per serving or whether to take a few extra minutes to prepare them from scratch.

The choice is yours. I have included recipes for both.

But here's the dilemma: Whenever you spend money to save time, you must spend time to make the money you spent to save time. Only you can decide whether it's worth it!

Time-Saving Tips

Here are a few tips for saving time in the kitchen:

❀ Preparation

Paint a chalkboard inside your pantry door, and write your weekly menu on the chalkboard. Make your grocery list from the menu. Check sales when making your menu to save money. Keep your pantry and freezer stocked with the basics, and whenever you run out of an item, write it on your chalkboard.

❀ Organization

Organize your kitchen into stations. Place all baking items in a cupboard next to the mixing bowls. Keep mixing appliances close by. Place cooking utensils in one drawer and the serving utensils in a separate drawer, both close to the stove. If you don't have an empty drawer, use a jar or crock to keep utensils at easy access. Also, keep seasonings, pans, and hot pads close to the stove. Store plastic containers, bags, plastic wrap, and foil in a drawer by the refrigerator. Keep serving dishes close to the sink and dishwasher. Place microwave-safe dishes in a cupboard next to the microwave.

❃ Buy Precooked Meats

Buy roast beef, turkey, or ham from your grocery deli. Ask for extra-thick slices so you can dice them for your recipes.

Fresh meat from the rotisserie or grill can include skinless chicken breasts, whole chickens, and half turkey breasts. Remove the skin, then shred or cut the meat as needed. Some stores offer seasoned grilled chicken strips. Packages are usually near the lunch meat section.

❃ No-Meat Meals

Save time by skipping the meat. Using beans, cheese, or eggs in the main dish can provide adequate protein for your meal and still be satisfying.

❃ Use Prepackaged Foods

Save preparation time by using refrigerator biscuits, frozen roll dough, quick rice and pastas, bagged salads and veggies, frozen vegetables, and canned vegetables, meats, and sauces.

❃ Speed Up Your Cleanup

Place a large bowl in the sink full of hot, sudsy water. Toss bowls and utensils in the sudsy water as you prepare the meal, and wash those dishes before dinner.

❃ Get Some Help

Speed up the preparation process by dividing up duties like peeling vegetables, grating cheese, opening cans, and so on. Assign each family member one night of the week to prepare dinner.

❃ Use Kitchen Gadgets and Tools

As mentioned earlier, innovation has led us to a life of convenience. Here are a few tools to save you time:

Kitchen Scissors—Use to cut bacon and chicken into strips and for cutting herbs and green onions.

Ice Cream Scoop—Use to scoop batter into muffin cups, to form meatballs and melon balls, and to measure cookie dough and mashed potatoes.

Food Processor—Makes chopping vegetables a breeze. Chop extras, pack them in zip-top bags, and store them in the refrigerator up to one week or freeze up to three months.

Pizza Cutter—Use to cut ham or other sandwich meats and cheeses into strips or cubes; to cut up pancakes, sandwiches, cooked meats, and other foods for little mouths to eat; to cut fudge and other candies; and to cut the dough for biscuits, rolls, and scones into squares.

Slow-Cooker—Prepare your dinner hours in advance and let it cook itself throughout the day.

Waffle Iron—Great for quesadillas, grilled cheese sandwiches, and hash browns.

Rolling Pin—Place crackers or walnuts in a bag; use the rolling pin to crush. Use a soup can or drinking glass as a substitute for a rolling pin.

Bottles and Containers—Fill bottles with olive or vegetable oil and cooking vinegars and keep them close to the stove. Use empty squeeze-top water bottles as dispensers for sauces, jam, maple syrup, even pancake batter.

Sour cream and whipped topping containers are great for storing leftovers.

Soup or vegetable cans can be used for unwanted meat drippings.

Cheese Grater—Use to grate carrots for salads and soups, potatoes for casseroles and potato salad, and pickles and eggs too!

Nut Chopper (Slap Style)—Use to chop onions, peppers, and celery with no mess.

Meat Mallet—Not only does it tenderize meat, but it thins the meat, making cooking time faster.

Make-Ahead Helps

Here are some recipes that save time and money by doubling a batch at dinnertime, cooking ahead, or making your own convenience foods.

Biscuit Mix and Refrigerator Biscuits

In a large mixing bowl, combine 12 C. all-purpose flour, 1 C. powdered milk, 3/4 C. sugar, 1/2 C. baking powder, and 2 T. salt. Store in a lidded container. To make biscuits: Combine 2 1/4 C. biscuit mix with 1/3 C. shortening or butter until crumbly. Stir in 2/3 C. water until dough is moistened. Roll and cut biscuits. Bake at 450 for 10–12 minutes.

For refrigerator biscuits: Follow recipe above. Roll dough into tube, wrap in plastic wrap, and refrigerate up to 1 week.

Freezer Dinner Rolls

Dissolve 1 pkg. yeast in 1/2 C. warm water. Mix in 1/3 C. sugar, 1/2 C. melted butter, 1 C. milk, 2 beaten eggs, 4 1/2 C. flour, and 1 tsp. salt. Knead to form soft dough. Place in greased bowl. Let rise until doubled. Roll out to 1-inch thickness. Cut dough into 1-inch squares. Roll squares in flour and place on baking sheet. Place in freezer until firm (1 hour).

Place frozen rolls loosely in freezer bags. Store up to 3 months. To cook, place frozen rolls on greased baking pan. Spray with cooking spray. Cover with plastic wrap and let rise in warm area until doubled (about 3 hours).

Bake at 350 for 15 minutes or until golden brown.

Pastas and Rice

Prepare pasta or rice according to package directions. Drain. Place in lidded container or zip-top bags. Refrigerate up to 5 days. Freeze up to 2 months.

Cook extra pasta or rice when making dinner. Refrigerate leftovers.

Lasagna and Pasta Casseroles

Prepare lasagna and pasta casseroles ahead of time. Do not cook pasta. Cover with foil and freeze until ready to bake. Bake with foil on until last 10 minutes of cooking time.

Rice-a-Roni

Break 1 C. angel hair pasta into 1-inch pieces. Blend with 1 C. rice. Pour 1 tsp. chicken bouillon, 1/2 tsp. Italian seasoning, and dash salt and pepper in zip-top bag. Store with rice mixture in airtight container.

Waffles, Pancakes, and French Toast

Double the breakfast batch of batter and cook up extra pancakes, waffles, or French toast. Freeze the leftovers. Just pop them in the toaster or microwave for an instant breakfast.

Spaghetti Sauce

Brown 1 lb. ground beef; drain fat. Stir in 2 15-oz. cans crushed tomatoes, 3 T. sugar, 1 T. Italian seasoning, and 1 tsp. garlic powder. Simmer until sauce deepens in color. Pour into quart jar. Refrigerate up to 1 week or freeze up to 1 year.

Meatless Sauce: Follow above recipe without meat.

Frozen Burritos

Spread 3–4 T. refried beans down the center of a flour tortilla. Sprinkle with 2–3 T. shredded cheddar cheese. Fold one side tortilla over to center. Fold top and bottom over fold (about 1 inch). Roll to make burrito. Repeat until you have used 1 15-oz. can refried beans.

Cooked Ground Beef

Cook ground beef with salt, pepper, and garlic powder. Place pan in refrigerator to cool meat. Remove fat from top of meat (this allows meat to keep juices). Place ground beef in freezer containers or bags. Freeze up to 1 year.

Slow-Cooked Chicken

Place chicken breasts in slow-cooker. Sprinkle with chicken bouillon, pepper, and paprika. Cover and cook on high 3 hours or low 6–7 hours. Wrap in foil and refrigerate up to 1 week or chop and place in freezer bags. Store in freezer up to 1 year.

Slow-Cooked Beef

Place a pot roast in slow-cooker. Sprinkle with au jus seasoning or beef bouillon. Cover and cook on high 3–5 hours or low 8–10 hours. Wrap in foil and refrigerate up to 1 week or chop and place in freezer bags. Store in freezer up to 1 year.

Slow-Cooked Pork

Follow recipe for Slow-Cooked Beef but use a pork roast. Using two forks, shred meat (do not chop). Freeze as above.

Frozen Vegetables

Place fresh vegetables in a metal strainer or colander. Lower into boiling water for time listed below. Immediately drop strainer into pot of cold water (blanch) for same amount of time as in boiling water. Drain water. Place vegetables in freezer bags. Write date on bag.

Peas—1 1/2 min. Corn—5–7 min. (Cut from cob before freezing.) **Broccoli—3 min. Carrots—5 min. Green beans—3 min. Hot and mild peppers—3 min. Spinach—2 min. Summer squash—3 min.**

Potatoes

Chop or shred potatoes. Rinse and blanch (see above) 5 minutes. Freeze up to 1 year. (Potatoes may brown; will lighten when cooked).

Boil potatoes in salted water; drain water. Cool thoroughly. Leave skins on. Refrigerate until ready to use. May store 3–4 weeks.

Throw 6–8 potatoes in to bake when you are preparing a casserole. Wrap potatoes in foil. Bake at 350 for 1 hour or at 425 for 45 minute. Do not unwrap. Refrigerate until ready to use. May store 3–4 weeks.

Frozen Fruit

Pat washed fruit dry. Spread out on tray or baking sheet. Freeze until firm (1 hour). Pack loosely in freezer bags. Write date on bag. Freeze up to 1 year. Fruits that freeze well:

Strawberries and other Berries, Apple Slices, Apricot Halves, Peach Halves, and Peach Slices

Sliced Strawberries. Sprinkle with sugar (3/4 C. per 1 quart fruit). Allow 15 minutes to draw out juice. Pack berries in freezer containers.

Notes & Tips

Every microwave oven cooks differently; you will need to adjust cooking times according to your microwave.

Microwave Meals

Broccoli Chicken

3 C. water
2 pkg. ramen noodles w/chicken seasoning
1 10-oz. pkg. frozen broccoli
1 10-oz. can chunk chicken or turkey
1/2 tsp. each salt and pepper

Cook water, ramen noodles, and broccoli in microwave-safe dish on high 3–4 minutes or until noodles are tender. Drain excess water. Sprinkle chicken seasoning over noodles. Stir in chicken or turkey, salt, and pepper. Cook 2 minutes.

Chicken and Vegetable Noodles: Substitute 1 12-oz. bag frozen mixed vegetables for the frozen broccoli.

Vegetable Beef and Noodles: In a microwave-safe dish, combine 1 lb. ground beef with salt, pepper, and garlic powder. Cook on high 3–4 minutes or until beef is no longer pink. Drain fat and set aside. In separate microwave-safe dish, cook noodles and vegetables according to above directions. Stir in cooked ground beef. Cook 2 minutes.

Chicken and Rice

1 8.5-oz. pkg. microwavable long-grain and wild rice (such as Uncle Ben's)
1 12-oz. pkg. frozen peas, thawed
1 10-oz. can chicken breast chunks

Empty rice package into microwave-safe dish. Stir in peas. Cook on high 2–3 minutes or until heated through. Add chicken and stir well. Cook 1 minute more.

Hamburger and Rice: Follow above directions, but replace chicken with 1 lb. cooked and drained ground beef.

Creamy Hamburger and Rice: Add 1 can cream of mushroom soup and 1/2 soup can milk to Hamburger and Rice.

Cheesy Ham and Rice: Follow recipe for Chicken and Rice but replace chicken with 1 1/2 C. diced ham. Stir in 1 C. shredded mozzarella cheese with diced ham. Continue as directed.

Twice-Baked Potatoes

4–6 baking potatoes
1/3 C. butter
1/4 C. milk
1/2 C. sour cream
1 C. shredded cheddar cheese + extra cheese
Salt and pepper to taste

Scrub and prick potatoes. Place on plate or microwave-safe dish. Cook 3 potatoes at a time on high 6–7 minutes or until potatoes are tender. Cut cooked potatoes lengthwise. Scoop potatoes into a mixing bowl. Mash potatoes and mix with butter, milk, sour cream, shredded cheese, salt, and pepper. Place potato skins on plate or dish. Fill skins with mashed potatoes. Sprinkle with additional shredded cheese. Microwave on high 1–2 minutes or until cheese is melted.

Stuffed Hot Dogs: Follow above recipe, but discard potato skins. Slit 8–12 hot dogs lengthwise partly but not all the way through. Open hot dogs and fill with mashed potato mixture. Continue directions for cooking as above.

Tater-Tot Casserole

1 32-oz. pkg. frozen tater-tots
1 lb. ground beef, cooked and drained
1 10-oz. can cream of mushroom soup
1/2 soup can milk
1 15-oz. can green beans, drained
Salt and pepper to taste

In a microwave-safe casserole dish, cook tater-tots on high 3 minutes or until thawed. Transfer onto plate. In original casserole dish, combine ground beef, soup, and milk. Fold in green beans. Season with salt and pepper. Spread tater-tots on top. Cook on high 3 minutes; stir and cook additional 2–3 minutes or until heated through.

Cheesy Tater-Tot Casserole: Stir 1 C. shredded cheddar cheese with green beans into above recipe.

Green Bean Casserole: Combine green beans, mushroom soup, and milk in casserole dish. Cook 2 minutes. Spread 2 C. French-fried onions over top. Cook additional 2–3 minutes or until casserole is hot and bubbly.

Chicken Enchilada Casserole

1 C. or 2 5-oz. cans chopped, cooked chicken
1 10-oz. can cream of chicken soup
1 C. sour cream
1 C. shredded cheddar cheese
1 4-oz. can diced green chiles
3 C. corn tortilla chips, slightly broken

In a microwave-safe casserole dish, combine chicken, soup, sour cream, shredded cheese, and green chiles. Microwave on high for 3 minutes. Remove from microwave; stir in corn tortilla chips. Return to microwave and cook on high 3 minutes or until heated through.

Cheese Enchilada Casserole: Spread 4 C. broken chips in microwave dish. Sprinkle with 1 C. shredded cheddar cheese. Pour 1 15-oz. enchilada sauce over chips and top with 1 C. shredded cheddar cheese. Cook according to directions above.

Super Quick Chili and Beans

1 lb. ground beef, cooked and drained
1 15-oz. can chili con carne
1 15-oz. can kidney beans
1 C. picante sauce or salsa
1/2 tsp. chili powder
Shredded cheddar cheese (opt.)
Finely diced onions

Combine ingredients in a microwave-safe dish. Cook on high 3 minutes. Stir and cook 3 minutes more. If desired, serve with a garnish of shredded cheese and diced onions.

IT IS BECOMING INCREASINGLY CLEAR THAT THE HOME AND FAMILY ARE THE KEY TO THE FUTURE.

HAROLD B. LEE

Nachos Supreme

1 lb. ground beef, cooked and drained (opt.)
1 bag corn tortilla chips
1 15-oz. can black beans or refried beans
2 C. shredded cheddar cheese
Sour cream
Salsa
2 tomatoes, chopped
1 green bell pepper, chopped
1/4 C. onion, diced
2 avocados, chopped
1 can olives, drained and sliced

Cook and drain ground beef. On individual plates, layer chips, ground beef, beans, and shredded cheese. Microwave on high 1 minute or until cheese is bubbly and melted. Top with sour cream, salsa, and desired toppings.

But ye will teach them to walk in the ways of truth and soberness; ye will teach them to love one another, and to serve one another.

Mosiah 4:15

Hot Layered Dip

1 15-oz. can refried beans
1/2 env. taco seasoning
2 ripe avocados
1/2 tsp. garlic salt
1 C. sour cream
2 C. shredded cheddar cheese
2 C. chopped lettuce
2 tomatoes, diced
Corn tortilla chips

In a microwave-safe dish, combine refried beans and taco seasoning; spread evenly. Mash avocados; stir in garlic salt and sour cream and spread over beans. Layer cheese, lettuce, and tomatoes on top. Microwave on high 2–3 minutes or until cheese is melted and bubbly. Serve with corn tortilla chips.

Meaty Hot Layered Dip: Follow above recipe but cook and drain 1 lb. ground beef. Combine with remaining 1/2 envelope of taco seasoning. Sprinkle meat over beans. Continue as directed.

2-Minute Omelets

8 eggs (2 eggs per omelet)
2 T. water
1 C. shredded cheddar cheese
1/2 C. cooked diced ham or crumbled bacon
1/4 C. diced green bell pepper
1/4 C. finely diced onion
Salt and pepper to taste

Combine egg and water until well blended. Spray 4 custard cups, 1/2-pint canning jars, or cocoa mugs with nonstick cooking spray. Pour 1/4 egg mixture into each prepared cup. Stir in cheddar cheese, ham, bell pepper, onion, salt, and pepper. Microwave on high for 1 minute; stir. Cook 1 to 1 1/2 minutes more or until eggs are completely set.

If that morning I whistled at my work,
it was because a great happiness filled my heart.
For I still had time, if I used it well.

Author Unknown

Breakfast Casserole

2 potatoes, peeled and shredded
Salt and pepper to taste
6 slices bacon
6 eggs, well beaten
2 T. milk
1 1/2 C. shredded cheddar cheese

Rinse shredded potatoes. Place in a microwave-safe casserole dish. Sprinkle with salt and pepper. Cook on high 2 minutes. Cut bacon into 1-inch strips. Stir into potatoes; cook on high 5 minutes. Stir in eggs, milk, and shredded cheese. Sprinkle with salt and pepper. Cook on high 1 minute.

Breakfast Burrito Casserole: In a microwave-safe dish, place 6 slices bacon (cut into 1-inch pieces) and 1/4 C. each diced onions and green bell peppers. Cook on high 2 minutes. Stir in 6 well-beaten eggs and 2 T. milk. Cook on high 2 minutes. Sprinkle with salt and pepper. Tear 3 flour tortillas into 2-inch pieces. Fold tortilla pieces and 1 1/2 C. shredded cheddar cheese into casserole. Cook on high 1 minute or until eggs are completely cooked. Serve with salsa.

Notes & Tips

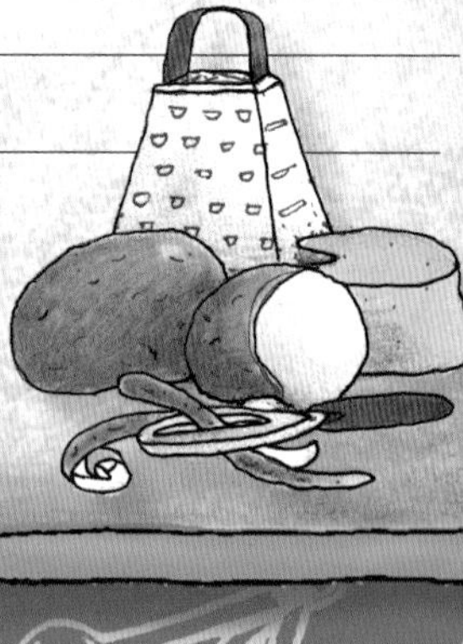

Slice foods thin or cut into smaller pieces for faster cooking times. Grated carrots in soups and stews cook faster and taste great.

Simply Soups

Simply Chicken Noodle Soup

2 T. butter
4 ribs celery, sliced 1/2 inch thick
1 onion, chopped
8 C. water, divided
2 tsp. chicken bouillon granules
1 tsp. each basil, oregano, salt, and pepper
1 lb. baby carrots, sliced 1/2 inch thick
2 5-oz. cans chicken chunks, undrained
12-oz. bag wide egg noodles

In a large pot over medium heat, melt butter. Cook celery and onion in butter until just tender, about 5 minutes. Pour in water and sprinkle with chicken bouillon and seasonings. Stir in carrots; bring to a boil. Add chicken and noodles; reduce heat and simmer 20 minutes before serving.

Only love can be divided endlessly and still not diminish.

Ann Morrow Lindbergh

Super Fast Chicken Vegetable Soup

1 12-oz. bag frozen vegetables
8 C. water
1 T. parsley flakes
2 pkg. chicken-flavored ramen noodles
2 5-oz. cans chicken chunks, undrained

Place vegetables and water in a soup pot. Bring to a boil over medium-high heat. Stir in parsley flakes and ramen noodles with seasoning. Cook noodles 3 minutes. Reduce heat to medium-low and stir in undrained chicken chunks. Heat through.

Super Fast Chicken Noodle Soup: Boil 8 C. water. Stir in 1 12-oz. bag wide egg noodles and 1 tsp. salt. Cook 7 minutes or until noodles are tender. Stir in 1 12-oz. bag frozen vegetables, 2 tsp. chicken bouillon, 1 T. parsley flakes, and 2 5-oz. cans undrained chicken chunks. Heat through.

Quick Chicken Alfredo Soup

1 14-oz. can chicken broth
1 12-oz. bag frozen stir-fry vegetables
2 10-oz. cans chicken breast chunks, drained
1 28-oz. jar Alfredo pasta sauce

In a soup pot, combine chicken broth and frozen vegetables. Sprinkle with salt and pepper to taste. Cover and cook over medium heat 5 minutes or until vegetables are just tender. Stir in chicken chunks and pasta sauce. Heat through. Sprinkle with Parmesan cheese.

Garlic Chicken Alfredo Soup: Add 1 1/2 tsp. garlic powder with chicken and pasta sauce.

Pasta Alfredo Soup: Cook 1 12-oz. package bow-tie or curly pasta according to package directions; drain. Stir pasta into cooked soup. Sprinkle with Parmesan cheese.

Potato-Sausage Toscana Soup

3 links sweet Italian sausage
2–3 slices bacon, diced
1 onion, diced
1 clove garlic, minced
2 14-oz. cans chicken broth, divided
2 baking potatoes, chopped (do not peel)
2 C. fresh kale, spinach, or frozen spinach
1 C. whipping cream

Remove sausage from casings; brown in skillet, breaking up, until cooked through. In a soup pot, cook bacon and onion over medium heat until onions are tender. Add garlic and cook 1 minute more. Add 1 can chicken broth and potatoes; simmer 15–20 minutes or until potatoes are tender. Stir in remaining chicken broth, sausage, kale or spinach, and cream. Simmer 5 minutes and serve.

Hamburger Soup

1 1/2 lb. ground beef
Salt and pepper to taste
4 ribs celery, sliced
1 yellow onion, chopped
4 C. hot water
2 C. frozen, fresh, or canned corn
2 tsp. beef bouillon granules
1 tsp. celery seed

In a large soup pot, brown beef with salt, pepper, celery, and onion over medium heat until meat is no longer pink. Stir in the water, corn, bouillon, and celery seed. Bring to a boil. Reduce heat; cover and simmer for 10–15 minutes or until vegetables are tender.

Creamy Hamburger Soup: Follow above recipe but stir 1 env. country gravy mix into cooked ground beef before adding water. Replace 2 C. water with 2 C. milk.

Cheeseburger Soup

1 lb. ground beef
1/2 tsp. each salt, pepper, and garlic powder
1 onion, diced
1/4 C. all-purpose flour
3 C. chicken broth
4 C. frozen hash-brown potatoes
2 C. shredded cheddar cheese
1 C. milk
1/2 C. sour cream
Sliced dill pickles (opt.)

In a large soup pot, cook beef with salt, pepper, garlic powder, and onion until meat is cooked. Stir in flour to form a smooth paste. Slowly stir in chicken broth. Add hash browns and bring to a boil. Reduce temperature; simmer 10 minutes. Stir in shredded cheese, milk, and sour cream. Heat through. Garnish with dill pickles.

Quick and Easy Minestrone Soup

1 onion, finely diced
1/4 C. butter
1/4 C. all-purpose flour
2 C. water
1 12-oz. bag frozen mixed vegetables
2 14.5-oz. cans Italian-style diced tomatoes
1 15-oz. can kidney beans
1 15-oz. can cannellini or navy beans
1 tsp. Italian seasoning
2 tsp. garlic powder
1/2 tsp. each salt and pepper

In a soup pot over medium heat, sauté onion in butter until onion starts to turn clear (do not brown). Reduce heat to low; stir in flour to form a smooth paste. Slowly stir in water. Add vegetables, tomatoes, and beans. Stir in Italian seasoning, garlic powder, salt, and pepper; cover and simmer over medium-low heat 5–6 minutes.

Easy Tomato Soup

2 T. butter, melted
2 T. all-purpose flour
2 8-oz. cans tomato sauce
2 C. water
Salt and pepper to taste

In a soup pot, melt butter. Stir in flour to make a smooth paste. Slowly stir in tomato sauce and water. Cook and stir over medium heat until soup boils and begins to thicken. Remove from heat. Cool slightly before serving. Salt and pepper to taste.

Tomato Vegetable Soup: Replace tomato sauce with 3 C. tomato-vegetable juice (such as V8) and decrease water to 1 C. Continue as directed above.

FAMILY ...it's about Time!

Creamy Onion Soup

1 onion, finely diced
1/4 C. butter
1/4 C. all-purpose flour
2 C. milk + 2 C. water
1 1/2 C. shredded sharp cheddar cheese
Salt and pepper to taste

In a soup pot over medium heat, sauté onion in butter until onion starts to turn clear (do not brown). Reduce heat to low; stir in flour to form a smooth paste. Slowly stir in milk and water. Bring to a boil, stirring often. Continue to cook and stir until thickened. Turn off heat. Stir in shredded cheese. Season with salt and pepper.

Creamy Zucchini Soup: Follow above directions but reduce onion to 1/4 C. Add 4 C. thinly sliced zucchini with milk and water. Bring to a boil, stirring often. Reduce heat; cover and simmer 5–7 minutes or until zucchini is just tender. Stir in shredded cheese until melted.

Summer Squash Bow-Tie Soup

2 C. water
6 C. chicken broth
2 1/4 C. (6 oz.) bow-tie pasta
2 C. yellow squash, finely diced
2 C. zucchini, finely diced
1 yellow onion, finely diced
1 T. fresh or dried parsley
1 T. Italian seasoning
1 T. fresh lemon juice (opt.)
1/2 tsp. each salt and ground black pepper
1/2 C. (2 oz.) grated Parmesan cheese

In a large soup pot, bring water and chicken broth to a boil. Add pasta and sprinkle with salt. Boil 8 minutes or until pasta is almost tender. Add yellow squash, zucchini, onion, seasonings, lemon juice, salt, and pepper. Boil 4 minutes more or until pasta is done and squash is tender. Sprinkle individual servings with Parmesan cheese.

Cabbage Soup

1 T. vegetable oil
1 yellow onion, finely diced
2 green onions, chopped (opt.)
2 carrots, peeled and shredded
2 celery ribs, diced small
2 garlic cloves, minced
3 14-oz. cans chicken broth
1/2 head green cabbage, thinly sliced
1 tsp. poultry seasoning
Salt and pepper to taste
2 tsp. white vinegar

In a soup pot, heat oil over medium-high heat. Add onions, carrots, celery, and garlic; cook and stir 5 minutes or until softened. Add broth and bring to a boil. Stir in cabbage, poultry seasoning, salt, and pepper. Cover and cook until cabbage is tender, about 15 minutes. Remove from heat; stir in vinegar. Season with salt and pepper.

Broccoli Soup

2 C. water
4 potatoes, peeled, chopped, and rinsed
1 tsp. chicken bouillon granules
1 broccoli branch, coarsely chopped
1 carrot, peeled and shredded
Salt and pepper to taste
1 10 3/4-oz. can cream of chicken soup
1 C. sour cream

In a soup pot, place water and chopped potatoes. Sprinkle with chicken bouillon. Spread broccoli and shredded carrots over potatoes. Sprinkle with salt and pepper. Cover and cook over medium-low heat for 15–20 minutes or until potatoes are tender. Gently mash vegetables. Stir in soup and sour cream. (If needed, thin soup with milk.) Heat through.

Cheesy Broccoli Soup: Replace cream of chicken soup with 2 C. shredded sharp or medium cheddar cheese. Stir and cook until cheese is melted. (Processed cheese, such as Velveeta, may also be used in this recipe.)

Baked Potato Soup

1/4 C. butter
1/4 C. flour
4 C. milk
3 potatoes, baked, peeled, and diced
2 green onions, thinly sliced
6–8 strips bacon, cooked and crumbled
1 C. shredded cheddar cheese
1/2 C. sour cream
Salt and pepper to taste

In a soup pot, melt butter. Add flour and stir until smooth and bubbly. Gradually add milk; stir constantly until sauce has thickened. Add potatoes and onions. Continue to cook, stirring constantly, until soup begins to bubble. Reduce heat. Add remaining ingredients; stir until cheese is melted.

WE LEARN TO COPE WITH THE PEOPLE OF THIS WORLD BECAUSE WE LEARN TO COPE WITH THE MEMBERS OF OUR FAMILY.

James Q. Wilson

Hash Brown Soup

1 16-oz. bag frozen hash-brown potatoes
2 C. water
Salt and pepper to taste
1 onion, finely diced
1/4 C. butter
1/4 C. all-purpose flour
2 C. milk
1 1/2 C. shredded sharp cheddar cheese

In a soup pot, place hash-brown potatoes and water; sprinkle with salt and pepper and bring to a boil. Reduce temperature to low and allow potatoes to simmer. In a separate pot, sauté onions in butter until onions start to turn clear (do not brown). Reduce heat to low; stir in flour to form a smooth paste. Slowly stir in milk. Add hash-brown potatoes and bring to a boil, stirring often. Continue to cook and stir until thickened. Turn off heat. Stir in shredded cheese.

Hash Brown and Bacon Soup: Follow above directions, but crumble 8–10 slices cooked bacon. Stir in crumbled bacon with the shredded cheddar cheese.

Spicy Corn Chowder

1 onion, finely diced
2 celery ribs, finely diced
1 jalapeño pepper, seeded and minced
2 garlic cloves, minced
3 T. butter
3 T. all-purpose flour
4 C. milk
1 16-oz. bag frozen super-sweet corn
1/4 tsp. each salt and black pepper
1/4 tsp. ground red pepper

In a soup pot, sauté onion, celery, jalapeño pepper, and garlic in butter over medium heat until tender. Stir in flour; cook 1 minute, stirring constantly. Slowly stir in milk, corn, and seasonings. Cook and stir until thickened (about 5 minutes).

For a milder chowder, omit jalapeño pepper and red pepper.

Chicken Corn Chowder: Add 1 C. chopped, cooked chicken chunks to above recipe.

Black Bean and Corn Soup

4 garlic cloves, minced
1 tsp. chili powder
1 T. olive oil
2 14.5-oz. cans diced tomatoes in juice
2 15-oz. cans black beans, drained
1 14-oz. can chicken broth
1 15-oz. can whole-kernel corn, drained
Salt and pepper to taste
1 C. water
1 T. fresh lime juice (opt.)

In a soup pot, sauté garlic and chili powder in olive oil over medium heat 1 minute or until you can smell the garlic. Add tomatoes, beans, broth, corn, salt, pepper, and water. Bring soup to a boil; simmer 2 minutes. Remove from heat; stir in lime juice and season with salt and pepper.

Serve with corn tortilla chips and lime wedges.

Taco Soup

2 lb. ground beef
1 env. taco seasoning
2 C. water
1 15-oz. can chili con carne with beans
1 15-oz. can whole-kernel corn, drained
1 14.5-oz. can stewed tomatoes
1 10-oz. can diced tomatoes/green chiles

In soup pot, cook beef over medium heat until no longer pink; drain. Add taco seasoning and mix well. Stir in remaining ingredients. Simmer, uncovered, for 15 minutes or until heated through, stirring occasionally.

Serve with choice of toppings:

Corn tortilla chips
Sour cream
Shredded cheddar or Monterrey Jack cheese
Chopped onions and/or peppers
Chopped fresh tomatoes
1 6-oz. can ripe olives, drained and sliced

Southwestern Pork Soup

2 T. olive oil or vegetable oil
1 lb. cubed pork stew meat
2 14-oz. cans chicken broth
2 C. black bean and corn salsa
1/2 env. taco seasoning
1/2 C. packed brown sugar

In a soup pot, heat oil over medium heat. Sear pork meat in hot oil until edges turn white. Pour just enough broth in soup pot to cover meat. Reduce heat to low, cover pot, and simmer 15 minutes. Add remaining broth, salsa, taco seasoning, and brown sugar. Cover and simmer 10 minutes more.

Serve with diced avocado, sour cream, and fresh cilantro.

This soup is also good served with corn tortilla chips and fresh-squeezed lime.

Easy Chili Beans

1 lb. ground beef
1/2 C. diced yellow onion
2 celery ribs, diced
1 15-oz. can pinto beans with liquid
1 15-oz. can kidney beans with liquid
1 14.5-oz. can diced tomatoes w/green chiles
1 14.5-oz. can crushed tomatoes
1 T. chili powder
1 tsp. cumin
1 tsp. sugar
1/2 tsp. each salt, pepper, and garlic powder

In soup pot, brown beef with onion and celery over medium heat until meat is done. Stir in remaining ingredients and simmer over medium-low heat 20 minutes.

If desired, serve with chopped fresh onions and shredded cheddar cheese as a garnish.

Easy White Chili

2 14.5-oz. cans chicken broth
2 15-oz. cans northern beans with liquid
2 10-oz. cans chicken breast chunks
1 4-oz. can diced green chiles
4 green onions, diced
1 tsp. each cumin and chili powder
1/2 tsp. each salt, pepper, and garlic powder

In a medium soup pot, combine all ingredients. Simmer over medium-low heat 15–20 minutes.

Serve with choice of toppings:

- Corn tortilla chips
- Sour cream
- Shredded Monterrey Jack cheese
- Lime wedges

You can use cooked turkey instead of chicken in this recipe.

Notes & Tips

Store pastas and rice in canning jars and canisters; it saves on opening bags during cooking and keeps them fresh longer.

Simply Salads

Seashell Salad

2 C. small seashell macaroni
1 C. mayonnaise or salad dressing
1 tsp. salt
1/2 tsp. paprika
1/4 C. onion, finely diced
3 celery stalks, chopped
1 C. finely diced dill pickle (opt.)
2 5-oz. cans tuna, drained
2 C. fresh or frozen peas

Cook seashell macaroni according to package directions; drain. In a medium mixing bowl, combine mayonnaise, salt, paprika, onion, celery, and pickles. Fold in tuna and peas. Chill before serving.

You can substitute chunk chicken or turkey for the tuna in this recipe.

In time of test, family is best!

Shrimp Salad

1 12-oz. pkg. small salad-roni
1 C. mayonnaise
1/4 C. sweet relish
1/4 C. hot dog relish
2 T. ketchup
2 T. Worcestershire sauce
1 rib celery, finely diced
2 6-oz. cans whole baby shrimp
Salt and pepper to taste

Cook pasta according to package directions; drain. In a medium mixing bowl, combine mayonnaise, relishes, ketchup, and Worcestershire sauce. Fold in celery and shrimp. Season with salt and pepper. Chill until ready to serve.

Crab Salad: Follow above recipe but substitute 1 C. chopped imitation crab meat for shrimp. Add 1 C. sliced cherry tomatoes and 1 can drained and sliced olives.

Greek Pasta Salad

1 12-oz. pkg. rainbow spiral pasta
1 C. mayonnaise
1 C. Italian dressing
1 C. grape or cherry tomatoes, halved
1 cucumber, peeled and chopped
1 C. ripe black olives, halved
1 C. pimento-stuffed green olives, halved
1/2 purple onion, sliced (opt.)
1 C. feta cheese (any flavor)

Cook pasta according to package directions; drain. Set pasta aside to cool. In a large bowl, combine mayonnaise and Italian dressing; stir in remaining ingredients. Fold in cooked and cooled pasta.

Smoked Sausage Pasta Salad: Follow above directions but add 1 lb. cooked and sliced smoked sausage.

Very Veggie Greek Pasta Salad: Add sliced zucchini and baby spinach leaves to recipe.

B.L.T. Pasta Salad

1 16-oz. package bow-tie pasta
1 12- to 16-oz. pkg. sliced bacon
1 1/2 C. Ranch-style salad dressing
1/2 C. diced green onion
2 cucumbers, peeled and chopped
2 tomatoes, chopped

Cook pasta according to package directions; drain. Cook the bacon over medium-high heat until browned and crisp. Remove from pan and drain on paper towels. In a large bowl, combine the Ranch dressing, green onion, cucumbers, and tomatoes. Fold in pasta. Refrigerate until ready to serve. Crumble bacon over the top just before serving.

You can substitute 1 C. crumbled feta cheese and 1 C. Italian dressing for the Ranch-style dressing in this recipe.

If desired, fold in 1 C. sliced black olives with the cucumbers and tomatoes.

Garden Pasta Salad

16 oz. rotini pasta
1 8-oz. bottle zesty Italian dressing
4 T. McCormick Salad Supreme Seasoning
1/2 C. sliced red onions
2 tomatoes, chopped
2 cucumbers, peeled and chopped
1 bell pepper, diced (opt.)
1 can ripe olives, drained and sliced
Sliced pepperoni (cut slices in half)

Cook pasta according to package directions; drain and cool. In a large bowl, stir remaining ingredients. Fold in cooled pasta. Cover and refrigerate until ready to serve.

Rejoice with your family in the beautiful land of life.

ALBERT EINSTEIN

Bow-Tie Chicken Salad

1 box bow-tie pasta
1 C. mayonnaise
1/4 C. white sugar
1/4 C. vinegar
2 C. chopped, cooked chicken
2 C. red grapes
1 15-oz. can pineapple tidbits, drained
1/2 C. chopped cashews (opt.)
1 C. craisins (opt.)
2 bunches green onions, chopped

Cook pasta according to package directions; drain. In a medium mixing bowl, combine mayonnaise, sugar, and vinegar. Stir in chicken, grapes, pineapple, nuts, craisins, and green onions. Fold in pasta until well coated. Refrigerate until ready to serve.

You may substitute 1 1/2 C. coleslaw dressing for the homemade dressing in this recipe.

Fritos Bean Salad

1 small bag iceberg salad
1 15-oz. can kidney beans, drained
2 tomatoes, diced
1 green bell pepper, diced
1 onion, diced
1 C. shredded cheddar cheese
1 16-oz. bottle Catalina salad dressing
1 bag Fritos corn chips

In a large bowl, combine all ingredients except salad dressing and chips. Just before serving, add dressing and chips and toss to mix thoroughly.

You may add sliced olives, hot peppers, chopped cucumbers, and/or rinsed and drained black beans to this recipe.

Variation: Reduce dressing to 1/2 bottle and add 1 C. sour cream. Mix well before tossing with salad.

Taco Salad

1 15-oz. can chili con carne
1 14.5-oz. can stewed tomatoes
1 C. mild or medium salsa
1 16-oz. can whole-kernel corn, drained (opt.)
Tortilla corn chips
Toppings of choice, such as:
shredded cheese, sour cream,
torn lettuce leaves, chopped tomatoes,
chopped onions, chopped cucumbers,
sliced black olives

In a medium saucepan, combine chili, stewed tomatoes, salsa, and corn. Cook over medium heat until warmed through. Place tortilla chips in individual dishes. Place 1 scoop of chili over chips and cover with toppings of choice.

Individual bags of Fritos corn chips may be used in place of tortilla chips. For easy cleanup and fun for kids, serve salad in the individual chip bags.

3-Bean Salad

1 15-oz. can cut green beans, drained
1 15-oz. can cut yellow beans, drained
1 15-oz. can red kidney beans, drained
1 15-oz. can whole-kernel corn, drained (opt.)
1/4 C. chopped green bell pepper
1 C. sliced purple onion
1/2 C. cider vinegar
1/3 C. vegetable oil
1/2 C. granulated sugar
1 tsp. salt
1 tsp. pepper

Rinse beans; drain. Combine beans, corn, green pepper, and sliced onion. In a separate bowl, whisk remaining ingredients; pour over bean mixture. Toss salad well and refrigerate until ready to serve.

This recipe can be prepared in the morning or even the night before and stored in the refrigerator until ready to serve.

Zucchini Salad

2 large tomatoes, sliced
2 medium zucchini, sliced
1 C. sliced mushrooms
1/2 C. sliced purple onion
1 15-oz. can red beans, rinsed and drained
1 C. Italian salad dressing
1 bag chopped romaine lettuce
1 bag garlic and cheese croutons

Combine tomatoes, zucchini, mushrooms, onion, and rinsed beans. Place in a large zip-top bag. Pour dressing over vegetables; toss well to coat. Cover and chill for at least 8 hours or overnight. When ready to serve, toss with romaine lettuce and croutons.

Easy Chef Salad

1 8-oz. pkg. sliced American cheese
1 8-oz. pkg. sliced provolone cheese
1 8-oz. pkg. sandwich ham slices
3 hard-boiled eggs
3 C. torn lettuce leaves
2 tomatoes, diced
2 cucumbers, peeled and diced
1 bottle French-style salad dressing

Cut cheeses and ham into 1/2- x 2-inch strips. Peel and chop eggs. Toss cheeses, ham, and eggs with vegetables. Just before serving, toss with french dressing until well coated.

Easy Garlic Bread Sticks: Slice a loaf of French bread in half lengthwise. Spread heavily with softened butter. Sprinkle with garlic salt, a dash of Italian seasoning, and Parmesan cheese. Toast a few inches from broiler 2 minutes or until edges start to turn golden brown (watch carefully). Slice bread into 2-inch strips. Serve with any salad from this section.

Chinese Salad

1 pkg. ramen noodles, crushed
1/4 C. sesame seeds
1/2 C. slivered almonds
1 T. white sugar
1/4 C. vinegar
1/3 C. vegetable oil
Chicken seasoning mix from ramen noodles
1 14-oz. bag coleslaw salad
1 C. chopped, cooked chicken
1/2 C. chopped celery
1 bunch green onions, chopped

Spread ramen noodles, sesame seeds, and almonds on a baking sheet. Toast at 350 for 10 minutes. In a jar, mix sugar, vinegar, oil, and seasoning; store in refrigerator until ready to serve. In a medium mixing bowl, toss coleslaw, chicken, celery, and green onions. Add toasted noodles, sesame seeds, almonds, and dressing just before serving. Toss and serve immediately for best flavor and crunch.

Raspberry Salad

1 16-oz. container cottage cheese
1 6-oz. pkg. raspberry Jell-O
3 C. fresh or frozen raspberries
1 8-oz. container whipped topping

In a medium bowl, combine cottage cheese and dry Jell-O; mix until Jell-O is dissolved. Fold in raspberries and whipped topping. Refrigerate until ready to serve.

Banana-Berry Salad

1 16-oz. container cottage cheese
1 6-oz. pkg. strawberry Jell-O
3 C. fresh or frozen strawberries, sliced
1 8-oz. container whipped topping
4–6 sliced bananas

Follow above directions. Fold in bananas with whipped topping. Refrigerate until ready to serve.

Green Grape Salad

8 C. seedless green grapes
1 8-oz. pkg. cream cheese
1/2 C. white sugar
1 tsp. vanilla
1 C. sour cream
4 oz. chopped pecans
2 T. brown sugar

Wash and dry grapes. In a large bowl, beat cream cheese, sugar, and vanilla until smooth. Mix in sour cream. Add grapes and mix until evenly incorporated. Sprinkle with brown sugar and pecans, mix again, and refrigerate until ready to serve.

Sweet Green Grape Salad: Replace sour cream with 1 8-oz. container whipped topping.

Red and Green Grape Salad: For a more colorful salad, use 4 C. green grapes and 4 C. red grapes.

Notes & Tips

When cooking a casserole, cook meat for another meal. Place frozen chicken in baking pan. Sprinkle with salt and pepper. Cover with foil. Bake at 350 for 1 hour.

Quick Casseroles

Chicken Divan

1 10 3/4-oz. can cream of chicken soup
1/2 C. mayonnaise or salad dressing
1 tsp. lemon juice
1/4 tsp. each salt and pepper
1 12-oz. bag frozen broccoli cuts
2 C. chopped, cooked chicken
1 C. shredded cheddar cheese
1 C. soft bread crumbs
1/4 C. butter, melted

In a 9x13 greased baking dish, combine soup, mayonnaise, lemon juice, salt, and pepper until well blended. Fold in broccoli and chicken; sprinkle with cheese. Combine bread crumbs and butter; sprinkle over top. Bake at 350° for 30 minutes or until cheese is hot and bubbly.

The family circle **should be at one and the same time** *a circle of friends.*

Neal A. Maxwell

Ritzy Chicken Strips

2 lbs. boneless, skinless chicken tenders
2 C. plain yogurt or sour cream
2 C. broken Ritz crackers
1 C. grated dry Parmesan cheese
1/4 C. parsley flakes
2 T. garlic powder
1 tsp. each salt and pepper
6–8 russet baking potatoes (opt.)

If desired, place 6–8 scrubbed potatoes in 425-degree oven to bake while preparing and baking chicken.

Dip chicken tenders in yogurt or sour cream and place in a greased 9x13 baking dish. Place broken crackers in a zip-top bag. Using a rolling pin or straight-sided drinking glass, roll over bag to crush crackers. Add Parmesan cheese, spices, salt, and pepper to bag. Shake bag to blend; sprinkle over chicken. Cover with foil. Bake at 425 for 30 minutes. Remove foil; cook an additional 10 minutes. Serve with potatoes.

If desired, heat 1 can cream of chicken soup with 1/2 soup can of milk over stove top until warm. Serve over chicken.

Wild Rice and Chicken Bake

4–6 small boneless, skinless chicken breasts
2 4.3-oz. boxes long-grain and wild rice mix
1 16-oz. bag frozen baby peas
2 T. butter, sliced into 4 pats
3 C. water

Place chicken breasts in greased 9x13 baking dish. Sprinkle seasoning mix from rice over chicken. Spread rice and frozen peas over chicken and dot with pats of butter. Pour water over top. Cover with foil and bake at 350 for 35 minutes. Remove from oven and allow rice to absorb water 5 minutes more before serving.

1 16-oz. bag frozen broccoli cuts may be substituted for the frozen peas in this recipe.

You can also add 1/2 C. slivered or sliced almonds to this recipe.

Curly Noodle Chicken Alfredo

3 C. (12 oz.) curly noodles
1 C. chopped, cooked chicken
1 12-oz. bag frozen broccoli florets, thawed
1 16-oz. jar Alfredo pasta sauce
1 C. shredded Parmesan cheese
3/4 C. Panko crispy bread crumbs
3 T. butter, melted

Cook curly noodles according to package directions; drain. Stir chicken, broccoli, Alfredo sauce, and cheese in a 9x13 baking dish. Stir in noodles. Combine bread crumbs and melted butter; sprinkle evenly over casserole. Bake uncovered at 375 for 25–30 minutes or until thoroughly heated and topping is golden.

You can substitute 1 C. chopped, cooked ham for the chicken in this recipe.

Cheesy Chicken Green Bean Casserole

1 16-oz. box 3-minute pasta
1 10 3/4-oz. can cream of chicken soup
1/2 soup can milk
1/4 tsp. each salt and pepper
2 C. chopped, cooked chicken
1 15-oz. can french-sliced green beans, drained
1/2 C. shredded American-cheddar cheese
1 2.8-oz. can french-fried onions

Cook pasta according to package directions (this pasta cooks in 3 minutes; do not overcook!). Drain. In 9x13 baking dish, mix soup, milk, salt, and pepper until well blended. Stir in chicken, green beans, noodles, and cheese. Sprinkle French-fried onions over top. Bake uncovered at 350 for 30 minutes or until cheese is hot and bubbly.

You can substitute 1 lb. cooked and drained ground beef for the chicken in this recipe. Substitute 1 can cream of mushroom soup for the cream of chicken soup.

Chicken Cordon Bleu Casserole

1 10-oz. can chicken breast chunks
1 C. chopped, cooked ham
1 10-oz. can cream of chicken soup
1/2 soup can milk
1 C. shredded Swiss or mozzarella cheese
1 2.8-oz. can french-fried onions

Spread chicken chunks and chopped ham in a lightly greased 9x13 baking dish. Combine soup, milk, and cheese. Pour over meat. Sprinkle French-fried onions over top. Bake at 350 for 30 minutes or until cheese is hot and bubbly.

The greatest joys of life are experienced in happy family relationships.

GORDON B. HINCKLEY

Broccoli Casserole

2 10-oz. pkg. frozen chopped broccoli
1 1/2 C. instant rice
1 10-oz. can cream of mushroom soup
1 16-oz. pkg. Velveeta cheese, shredded
1 soup can filled with milk
1/4 C. butter, melted
1/2 tsp. each salt and pepper

Spread broccoli and rice evenly in a greased 9x13 baking dish. In a mixing bowl, combine soup, shredded cheese, milk, melted butter, salt, and pepper until well blended. Spread over broccoli-rice mixture. Tightly cover with foil. Bake at 350 for 30 minutes or until cheese is hot and bubbly.

You can substitute 1 6-oz. box chicken-flavored stuffing mix with seasoning for the instant rice in this recipe.

You can add 2 C. chopped, cooked chicken or turkey to this recipe. Spread chicken or turkey chunks in with broccoli and rice mixture. Continue as directed.

Tuna Noodle Bake

1 16-oz. box 3-minute pasta
1 10-oz. can cream of chicken/celery soup
1/2 soup can milk
2 5-oz. cans tuna, drained
2 C. frozen peas, thawed
Salt and pepper to taste
Dash of paprika
3 C. crushed potato chips (opt.)

Cook pasta according to package directions (this pasta cooks in 3 minutes; do not overcook!). In a 9x13 baking dish, combine soup, milk, tuna, peas, salt, and pepper. Fold in noodles. Sprinkle with paprika and crushed potato chips (if desired). Bake at 400 for 15 minutes or until chips start to brown.

You can substitute 1 15-oz. can French-sliced green beans (drained) for the green peas in this recipe.

Cheesy Tuna Noodle Bake: Stir in 1 C. shredded cheddar or processed cheese over casserole before baking.

Sausage Rice

1 lb. bulk pork sausage
2 stalks celery, coarsely chopped
1 large onion, coarsely chopped
1 6-oz. box long-grain and wild rice mix
2 C. chicken broth
1 10-oz. can cream of mushroom soup
1 C. shredded cheddar cheese (opt.)

Cook sausage with salt and pepper to taste in a skillet over medium-high heat until well browned. Drain fat. In a 9x13 baking dish, combine browned sausage with celery, onion, rice mix, broth, soup, and cheese. Cover with foil. Bake at 375 for 30 minutes or until rice is tender. Stir casserole before serving.

Hamburger Rice: Replace sausage with 1 lb. ground beef. Continue as directed.

NO SUCCESS CAN COMPENSATE FOR FAILURE IN THE *Home*

DAVID O. MCKAY

One-Step Lasagna

1 lb. lean ground beef *
1/2 tsp. each salt, pepper, and garlic powder
4 C. spaghetti sauce, divided
1 16-oz. container cottage cheese
1 T. parsley flakes (opt.)
10 lasagna noodles, uncooked
1 C. water
2 C. mozzarella cheese, divided
1/2 C. Parmesan cheese

In a mixing bowl, combine ground beef, salt, pepper, garlic powder, 2 C. spaghetti sauce, cottage cheese, and parsley flakes (if desired). Spread 1 C. spaghetti sauce in a 9x13 baking dish. Arrange 5 uncooked lasagna noodles over sauce. Spread 1/2 meat mixture over noodles. Sprinkle 1 C. mozzarella cheese and Parmesan cheese over meat. Add a second layer of 5 lasagna noodles and remaining meat mixture. Pour 1 C. water and remaining spaghetti sauce over meat. Sprinkle with remaining cheese. Tightly cover with foil. Bake at 350 for 45–50 minutes.

* Meat sauce or extra cheeses may replace ground beef.

Cheeseburger Pie

1 1/2 lb. lean ground beef
1/4 C. diced onion
Salt and pepper to taste
1/4 C. small diced dill pickles (opt.)
1/2 C. mayonnaise or salad dressing
1/2 C. ketchup
1 T. yellow mustard
1 C. shredded American cheese
1 8-oz. can refrigerated crescent dough

Brown ground beef with onion, salt, and pepper until thoroughly cooked; drain. Spoon into a 9x13 baking dish. Stir in pickles, mayonnaise, ketchup, and mustard. Sprinkle with cheese. Unroll dough; press into 12x8-inch rectangle. Cut into 6 squares; place on top of cheese. Bake at 375 for 20–25 minutes or until rolls are deep golden brown.

If desired, lift baked squares and top with shredded iceberg lettuce and sliced tomatoes; for onion lovers, top with sliced purple onions. Replace baked squares and serve.

Sloppy Joe Pie

2 lb. ground beef
1 onion, finely diced
1/2 env. sloppy joe seasoning mix
1 12-oz. bag matchstick carrots (opt.)
2 15-oz. cans crushed tomatoes
1/2 C. tomato ketchup
2 T. yellow mustard
3 T. white sugar
1 pkg. giant refrigerator biscuits

Brown ground beef with onion and salt and pepper to taste; drain. Spoon into a 9x13 baking dish. Stir in seasoning mix, carrots, tomatoes, ketchup, mustard, and sugar. Bake at 350 for 15 minutes. Top with biscuits and bake 15 more minutes.

DO YOUR PART TO DEVELOP REAL FAMILY UNITY AND SOLIDARITY. IN SUCH HOMES THERE IS NO GENERATION GAP.

Ezra Taft Benson

Shepherd's Pie

1 1/2 lb. lean ground beef
1/4 C. small diced onions
Salt and pepper to taste
1 16-oz. bag frozen mixed vegetables
1 10 3/4-oz. can cream of mushroom soup
2 C. prepared mashed potatoes

Over medium-high heat, brown ground beef with onion, salt, and pepper until thoroughly cooked; drain. Spoon beef and onions into a 9x13 baking dish. Stir in frozen vegetables and cream soup. Spread potatoes over top. Bake uncovered at 350 for 30 minutes.

Mashed Potato Pie: Combine the 2 C. mashed potatoes with 2 C. shredded cheddar cheese and 1 C. sour cream. Spread in 9x13 baking dish. Sprinkle with salt and pepper and 1 lb. cooked and crumbled bacon. Bake as directed above. Garnish with sour cream and chopped green onions or chives.

Macaroni Beef Bake

1 16-oz. box 3-minute macaroni
1 lb. extra-lean ground beef
1 C. chopped onion
Salt and pepper to taste
2 14.5-oz. cans diced tomatoes, undrained
2 C. shredded cheddar cheese

Cook pasta according to package directions (this pasta cooks in 3 minutes; do not overcook!). Drain pasta. Brown ground beef with onion, salt, and pepper over medium-high heat 5–7 minutes or until thoroughly cooked; drain. Spoon beef and onions into a 9x13 glass baking dish. Stir in tomatoes and shredded cheese. Bake uncovered at 350 for 30 minutes.

Macaroni Chili Bake: Combine cooked and drained macaroni with 1 15-oz. can chili con carne, 1 15-oz. can drained whole-kernel corn, 1 C. sour cream, and 1 C. shredded cheddar cheese. Bake as directed above.

Tin-Foil Casserole

2 lb. lean ground beef
1 onion, finely diced
1/2 tsp. each salt, pepper, and garlic powder
3 C. shredded frozen hash browns
1 bag matchstick carrots
1 12-oz. bag frozen peas
Salt and pepper to taste

Cut a piece of foil twice the length of a 9x13 baking dish. Center the foil in baking dish so foil extends evenly past ends of dish. In a mixing bowl, combine ground beef, diced onion, salt, pepper, and garlic powder until well blended. Press meat evenly in foil-lined baking dish. Spread hash browns, carrots, and peas evenly over meat. Sprinkle with salt and pepper to taste. Fold ends of foil over vegetables and seal all edges. Bake at 375 for 30 minutes.

Wherefore, my beloved brethren, let every man be swift to hear, slow to speak, slow to wrath.

James 1:19

Bean Casserole

1 1/2 lb. lean ground beef
8 slices bacon, chopped
1/2 C. diced onions
1/2 C. diced green bell pepper
1/2 C. brown sugar
1/2 C. ketchup
3 T. yellow mustard
1/2 tsp. each salt and pepper
3 15-oz. cans pork and beans, drained
1 15-oz. can kidney beans, drained

In a 9x13 baking dish, combine *uncooked ground beef and bacon with onions, peppers, brown sugar, ketchup, mustard, salt, and pepper until well blended. Stir in beans. Bake uncovered at 375 for 30 minutes. Before serving, stir to break up ground beef.

*If desired, ground beef and bacon may be cooked before combining all ingredients.

Meatloaf Casserole

1 1/2 lb. lean ground beef or ground turkey
1 6-oz. box stuffing mix (any flavor)
2 large eggs, well beaten
1 8-oz. can tomato sauce
2 T. Worcestershire sauce
1 12-oz. bag frozen mixed vegetables
1 10-oz. can cream of mushroom soup
1/2 soup can milk
1 C. sour cream (opt.)
1 C. shredded cheddar cheese

In a mixing bowl, combine ground beef or turkey, stuffing mix, eggs, tomato sauce, and Worcestershire sauce until well blended. Spray a 9x13 baking dish with nonstick cooking spray (if using turkey meat, spray heavily). Press meat mixture into baking dish. Spread frozen vegetables over meat mixture. In a separate bowl combine soup, milk, and sour cream (if desired). Pour over vegetables and meat. Sprinkle with shredded cheese. Bake at 350 for 30–40 minutes or until meat is cooked through.

Meatloaf Muffins

2 lb. lean ground beef or ground turkey
1 6-oz. box stuffing mix (any flavor)
2 large eggs, well beaten
1 10 3/4-oz. can cream of mushroom soup
1/2 soup can milk
Ketchup for topping

In a mixing bowl, combine all ingredients except ketchup. Spray muffin tin with cooking spray (if using turkey, spray heavily) or line muffin cups with paper liners. Press meat mixture into muffin cups. Bake at 375 for 25 minutes. Spread ketchup over tops of muffins. Bake an additional 10 minutes.

Tangy Meatloaf Muffins:
Replace cream of mushroom soup with 1 8-oz. can tomato sauce and 1/2 C. water. Continue as directed.

Taco Casserole

1 1/2 lb. lean ground beef
1/2 tsp. each salt, pepper, and garlic powder
1 15-oz. can chili con carne
1 15-oz. can whole-kernel corn, drained
1 6.5-oz. can ripe olives, drained
1 C. sour cream
2 C. shredded cheddar cheese
3 C. corn tortilla chips, slightly crumbled

Brown ground beef with salt, pepper, and garlic powder until thoroughly cooked; drain. Spoon beef into a 9x13 glass baking dish. Stir in remaining ingredients. Bake uncovered at 350 for 30 minutes.

Serve with sour cream, salsa, shredded lettuce, and chopped tomatoes and peppers.

For a more low-fat recipe, substitute 1 dozen corn tortillas, torn into small pieces, for the corn tortilla chips.

Quick and Easy Beef Enchiladas

1 20-oz. can red enchilada sauce
1 20-oz. box frozen beef taquitos, thawed
1 16-oz. can refried beans (opt.)
1 1/2 C. shredded Mexican blend cheese, divided
1/2 C. chopped onions (opt.)

Pour 1/2 of the enchilada sauce into a lightly greased 9x13 baking dish. Place taquitos over enchilada sauce. If desired, spread refried beans over taquitos. Sprinkle 1/2 of the shredded cheese over taquitos or beans. If desired, sprinkle with onions. Cover with remaining sauce.

Bake uncovered at 375 for 30 minutes or until heated through. The last 10 minutes of baking, top with remaining cheese.

Serve with sour cream, salsa, shredded lettuce, chopped tomatoes, peppers, olives, and other toppings of your choice.

Spicy Chicken Enchilada Casserole

2 5-oz. cans chicken breast chunks
1 tsp. chili powder
8 corn tortillas, torn into 2-inch pieces
1 10-oz. can cream of chicken soup
1 C. sour cream
1 C. shredded Monterrey Jack cheese
1 10-oz. can diced tomatoes and green chiles

Combine all ingredients in a 9x13 baking dish. Bake at 350 for 30 minutes.

Green Chile Chicken Enchilada Casserole: Follow above recipe but omit chili powder and replace diced tomatoes and chiles with 2 4-oz. cans diced green chiles.

You can substitute 1 lb. cooked and drained ground beef for the chicken breast chunks in this recipe. If so, replace Monterrey Jack cheese with 1 C. shredded cheddar cheese.

Cornbread Casserole

1 lb. lean ground beef, uncooked
1/2 tsp. each salt, pepper, and garlic powder
1 15-oz. can red enchilada sauce
1 15-oz. can whole-kernel corn, drained
1 8-oz. pkg. cornbread mix

In a 9x13 glass baking dish, combine ground beef, salt, pepper, garlic powder, enchilada sauce, and corn. In a separate bowl, prepare cornbread batter as directed. Spread over meat mixture. Bake at 350 for 30 minutes or until meat is thoroughly cooked.

Cheesy Cornbread Casserole: Follow above recipe, but sprinkle 1 C. shredded cheddar cheese over meat mixture before spreading cornbread batter. Continue as directed.

Earn the respect and confidence of your children through your loving relationship with them.

Howard W. Hunter

Notes & Tips

Purchase bottled minced garlic.
It is easy to use and can be stored for
several months in the refrigerator.

Skillet Dinners

Creamy Chicken and Dumplings

1 can cream of chicken soup
1 soup can of milk
2 C. cooked, chopped chicken breast
5 chopped green onions
1 C. shredded cheddar cheese (opt.)
10 refrigerator biscuits

In a large skillet, combine soup and milk. In a small bowl, combine chicken, onions, 1/2 C. soup from skillet, and cheese (if desired). Press biscuits to flatten. Place 1/4 C. chicken mixture in center of each biscuit. Fold over and seal biscuit edges with fork. Place dumplings evenly in soup mixture. Cover with a tight-fitting lid and cook over medium-low heat for 10 minutes. Turn dumplings and cook an additional 5–10 minutes or until dumplings are done. Serve with soup mixture spooned over dumplings.

Chicken Pot Pie

1/3 C. butter + butter for spreading
1/3 C. chopped onion
1/3 C. all-purpose flour
1/4 tsp. each salt and pepper
1 3/4 C. chicken broth
1/2 C. milk
2 1/2 C. chopped, cooked chicken
2 C. frozen mixed vegetables, thawed
6 home-style flour tortillas

Melt butter in a large skillet or saucepan. Add onion; cook and stir over medium heat until onions are tender. Stir in flour, salt, and pepper until well blended. Gradually stir in broth and milk, cooking and stirring until thickened and bubbly. Stir in chicken and vegetables. Heat through. Meanwhile, spread softened butter over tortillas. Place tortillas on a baking sheet. Using a pizza cutter, cut tortillas into 1/2-inch strips. Broil tortilla strips 2–3 minutes or until golden brown. Spoon chicken soup into individual bowls. Top each soup bowl with toasted tortilla strips.

Chicken Parmesan

1 T. olive oil
2 lb. boneless, skinless chicken breasts
1 C. spaghetti sauce
4 C. grated Parmesan cheese, divided
1/2 C. grated mozzarella cheese

In a large skillet, heat oil over medium-high heat. Place chicken in hot oil and brown on both sides. Reduce heat to low. Spread sauce and 1/4 C. Parmesan cheese over chicken. Cover and cook 15–20 minutes or until chicken is cooked through. Sprinkle remaining cheese on top. Cover and let stand for 5 minutes or until cheese is melted.

Serve with pasta or rice and green salad.

Family life should be a time of happiness and joy that children can look back on with fond memories.

Ezra Taft Benson

Red Pepper Tortellini Alfredo

2 9-oz. pkgs. refrigerated meat-filled tortellini
1 8-oz. jar roasted red sweet peppers
1 C. Alfredo sauce
1 tsp. dried basil
3 T. grated dry Parmesan cheese
1/2 tsp. ground black pepper

Cook tortellini according to package directions. Drain and set aside. Meanwhile, drain sweet peppers and cut into 1/2-inch strips. In a large skillet, heat Alfredo sauce. Stir in basil, Parmesan cheese, black pepper, and tortellini. Reduce heat and add sweet peppers. Simmer for 5 minutes, stirring often.

You can substitute chopped sun-dried tomatoes (drained) for the roasted red peppers in this recipe.

Bacon and Avocado Bow-Tie Pasta

8 oz. bow-tie pasta
6 slices bacon, cooked and crumbled
3 cloves garlic, minced
2 medium avocados, coarsely chopped
1 tsp. dried basil
2 T. lemon juice
Salt and pepper to taste
1/2 C. grated Parmesan cheese

Cook pasta according to package directions. Drain and set aside. In a large skillet, cook bacon over medium-high heat. Drain bacon fat and crumble bacon. Add garlic and cook for 30 seconds. Stir in pasta, chopped avocados, basil, lemon juice, salt, and pepper. Sprinkle with cheese.

Spicy Chicken Fajitas

2 T. vegetable oil, divided
1 large green bell pepper, chopped
1 onion, chopped
1 lb. chicken breast strips
1/2 C. water
1/2 pkg. fajita seasoning mix
3 medium firm tomatoes, chopped
10 flour tortillas
Sour cream
Grated cheddar cheese
Salsa

In a large skillet, heat 1 T. oil over medium-high heat. Stir-fry peppers and onions in hot oil until tender. Transfer vegetables to another dish. Stir-fry chicken in remaining oil until edges turn white. Reduce heat. Stir in 1/2 C. water and seasoning mix. Cover, reduce heat, and simmer 10 minutes. Add peppers, onions, and tomatoes. Warm through. Divide into warmed tortillas and serve with sour cream, cheese, and salsa.

Egg and Rice Tortilla Wraps

1 4.3-oz. pkg. chicken-flavor rice-a-roni
8 large eggs
2 T. milk
Salt and pepper to taste
10 flour tortillas
Salsa (opt.)

In a large skillet, prepare rice-a-roni according to package directions. Meanwhile, in a mixing bowl, whisk eggs, milk, salt, and pepper. When rice is completely cooked, remove from skillet. Spray skillet with nonstick cooking spray. Cook egg mixture over medium heat, continually stirring until done. Fold rice into scrambled eggs. Warm tortillas in microwave. Spoon egg-rice mixture down centers of tortillas and roll up.

If desired, serve with salsa.

Vegetable Lo-Mein

8 oz. spaghetti or fettuccine noodles
1 env. chow mein sauce mix
1/2 cabbage head, sliced
1 onion, chopped
4 celery ribs, sliced
2 T. olive oil

Cook pasta according to package directions. Drain and set aside. Meanwhile, make chow mein sauce mix according to package directions. Set aside. Heat oil in a large skillet over medium-high heat. Stir-fry cabbage, onion, and celery in hot oil until tender. Stir in sauce mix and drained vegetables. Reduce heat. Cover and simmer 2–3 minutes or until sauce thickens. Stir in pasta until well coated. Heat through.

You can add 1 lb. chicken breast strips to this recipe; stir-fry with vegetables.

Sesame Chicken and Rice

1 lb. chicken breast strips
1 T. + 2 T. soy sauce
1/4 C. apple cider vinegar
1/3 C. thinly sliced green onions
3 T. each honey, brown sugar, and sesame oil
1 T. grated fresh ginger
1/4 C. each flour and cornstarch
3 T. olive oil
2 T. sesame seeds
2 C. long-grain white rice, cooked

Place chicken and 1 T. soy sauce in a zip-top bag. In a medium bowl, combine 2 T. soy sauce, vinegar, green onions, honey, brown sugar, sesame oil, and ginger. Set aside. Sift flour and cornstarch and pour into bag; shake to coat chicken. Heat oil in a large skillet over medium-high heat. Stir-fry chicken tenders 4–5 minutes, or until no longer pink. Stir in sauce mixture and sesame seeds until bubbly and thickened. Serve over cooked rice.

Chicken, Broccoli, and Brown Rice

1 T. olive oil
1 lb. chicken breast strips
1/2 tsp. minced garlic
1 1/2 C. chicken broth
1 bunch broccoli, broken into florets
Salt and pepper to taste
1 1/2 C. instant brown rice
1 oz. grated Parmesan cheese (opt.)

Heat oil in a large skillet over medium-high heat. Stir-fry chicken strips 4–5 minutes, or until no longer pink. Add garlic, broth, broccoli, salt, and pepper. Bring to a boil. Stir in brown rice. Reduce heat to low. Cover and simmer 5 minutes. Sprinkle Parmesan cheese on top and serve.

You can substitute 1 lb. thinly sliced boneless beef strips for the chicken in this recipe. Replace chicken broth with beef broth.

Tuna Rice Skillet

1 1/2 C. white rice
2 5-oz. cans tuna, drained
1 14.5-oz. can green beans, drained (opt.)
1 can cream of mushroom soup
1/2 soup can of milk

In a large skillet or saucepan with tight-fitting lid, cook rice according to package directions. Stir in tuna, beans (if desired), soup, and milk.

You can substitute 1 C. frozen peas for the green beans in this recipe.

Bring up your children in *the love and fear* **of the Lord**

Brigham Young

Tuna Gravy and Waffle Biscuits

2 C. biscuit mix
1 C. milk
1 egg
2 T. vegetable oil
2 5-oz. cans tuna, drained
1 can cream of mushroom soup
1/2 soup can of milk

In a medium bowl, combine biscuit mix, milk, egg, and oil until just moist. Heat waffle iron. Spray waffle iron with nonstick cooking spray. Spread batter into iron. Cook 2–3 minutes or until waffles are golden. Repeat until all waffles are cooked. Meanwhile, in a skillet or saucepan, combine tuna, soup, and milk. Heat through. Place waffles on individual plates and smother with tuna gravy.

You can substitute 1 lb. cooked and drained ground beef for the tuna in this recipe.

Easy Beef and Broccoli Stir-Fry

2 C. instant white rice, uncooked
1 T. vegetable oil
1 lb. beef stir-fry strips
2 C. frozen broccoli florets
1/4 C. hoisin sauce
1/4 C. balsamic vinaigrette or Catalina salad dressing
1 T. grated ginger root

Cook rice as directed. Meanwhile, in a large nonstick skillet, heat oil over medium-high heat. Add beef; stir-fry 3 minutes or until evenly browned. Add broccoli, hoisin sauce, dressing, and ginger root; stir. Cover. Simmer over low temperature 5 minutes or until heated through.

Serve over the rice.

Beef and Broccoli Noodle Bowl

1/2 lb. linguine, uncooked
1 T. vegetable oil
1 lb. beef sirloin steak, thinly sliced
1 C. broccoli florets
1/2 C. matchstick carrots
1/2 C. beef broth
1/3 C. hoisin sauce
1/4 C. balsamic vinaigrette or Catalina salad dressing
1 T. grated ginger root

Cook pasta as directed; drain. Meanwhile, in a large non-stick skillet, heat oil over medium-high heat. Add beef, broccoli, and carrots; stir-fry 4 minutes or until meat is evenly browned. Stir in broth, hoisin sauce, dressing, and ginger root. Cover. Reduce temperature to low; simmer 3 minutes or until vegetables are crisp-tender, stirring occasionally. Stir in cooked linguine.

Beef and Vegetable Ramen Noodles

1 1/2 lb. ground beef
1/3 C. finely diced onions
Salt and pepper to taste
3 C. water
2 3-oz. pkgs. ramen noodles w/beef seasoning packets
2 C. frozen mixed vegetables, thawed

In a large skillet, brown ground beef with onions, salt, and pepper. Drain fat. Add water and bring to a boil. Stir in ramen noodles, seasoning packets, and frozen vegetables. Cook for 3 minutes or until noodles are tender.

Creamy Beef and Noodles: Follow above recipe but reduce to 2 C. water. After noodles are cooked, stir in 1 can cream of mushroom soup. If desired, substitute 1 15-oz. can green beans (drained) for frozen vegetables.

Quick and Easy Beef Stroganoff

12 oz. wide egg noodles
1 1/2 lb. ground beef
1 onion, chopped (opt.)
1/2 tsp. each garlic powder, salt, and pepper
1 can cream of mushroom soup
1/2 soup can of milk
1 C. sour cream
2 T. Worcestershire sauce

Cook pasta according to package directions; drain. In a large skillet, brown ground beef, onion, salt, pepper, and garlic powder; drain. Stir in soup, milk, sour cream, and Worcestershire sauce. Heat through. Serve over egg noodles.

FAMILY

a haven against the storms and struggles of life.

Spencer W. Kimball

Hamburger Gravy and Rice

1 1/2 lb. ground beef
1 onion, chopped (opt.)
Salt and pepper to taste
1/2 tsp. garlic powder
3 C. water
1 1/2 C. long-grain white rice
1 can cream of mushroom soup
1/2 soup can of milk
1 C. sour cream
2 T. Worcestershire sauce

In a large skillet, brown ground beef and onion with salt, pepper, and garlic powder. Drain all but 1 T. fat. Add water and bring to a boil. Stir in rice. Reduce heat to low. Cover and simmer 20 minutes or until rice is done. Stir in soup, milk, sour cream, and Worcestershire sauce. Heat through. You may substitute quick-cooking rice for the long-grain rice in this recipe.

Skillet Spanish Rice

6 slices bacon
1/2 C. finely diced onion
1/2 C. finely diced green bell pepper
1 1/2 C. long-grain white rice
3 C. water
1/2 tsp. salt
1 tsp. chili powder
1 C. mild salsa
1 C. grated cheddar cheese (opt.)

Cook bacon over medium-high heat. Remove bacon, crumble, and set aside. Do not drain bacon fat. Add onions, peppers, and rice to bacon fat. Cook 2–3 minutes or until rice starts to turn golden brown. Add water, salt, chili powder, and salsa. Bring mixture to a boil. Reduce heat to low, cover, and simmer 20 minutes or until rice is tender. Stir in crumbled bacon and sprinkle cheese over top. Cover and allow cheese to melt (about 5 minutes).

You can add 1 lb. cooked and drained ground beef to this recipe when you stir in the water and salsa.

Chili Macaroni in a Skillet

2 C. macaroni noodles
1 15-oz. can chili con carne with beans
1 15-oz. can whole-kernel corn, drained
1 C. sour cream
1 C. grated cheddar cheese

Cook pasta according to package directions. Drain. In a large skillet, combine noodles, chili, corn, sour cream, and grated cheese. Cook and stir over medium heat until cheese is melted.

Tomato Mac-and-Cheese: Follow above directions, but substitute 1 15-oz. can undrained whole tomatoes for chili beans. Omit sour cream. Sprinkle with salt and pepper.

IF THERE IS TO BE A RETURN TO OLD AND SACRED VALUES,
IT MUST BEGIN IN THE HOME.

Gordon B. Hinckley

Cheesy Macaroni and Franks

2 C. macaroni noodles
1 pkg. hot dogs, sliced diagonally in 1/2-inch pieces
1/4 C. butter
1/4 C. all-purpose flour
1 C. milk
2 C. grated cheddar cheese

Cook pasta according to package directions. Drain and set aside. In a large skillet, stir-fry sliced hot dogs over medium-high heat until edges are browned. Remove hot dogs. Melt butter in skillet. Add flour and stir until well blended. Gradually stir in milk. Cook and stir over medium heat until thickened and bubbly. Stir in cheese until melted. Return hot dogs and macaroni to skillet and warm through.

You can substitute 2 boxes packaged macaroni and cheese for the homemade version in this recipe.

Beef and Potato Skillet Dinner

1 lb. ground beef
1 onion, chopped
Salt and pepper to taste
1/2 tsp. garlic powder
3 potatoes, peeled and thinly sliced
1 14.5-oz. can green beans, drained (opt.)
1 can cheddar cheese soup
1/2 soup can of milk

In a large skillet, brown ground beef and onion with salt, pepper, and garlic powder. Drain fat. Add potatoes and cook over medium-high heat, stirring occasionally until potatoes are tender. Reduce heat to low. Stir in green beans (if desired), soup, and milk. Cover and simmer 3–4 minutes.

You can use 1 C. frozen peas in this recipe instead of the green beans.

Ham and Garlic Potatoes

8–10 red potatoes, washed and quartered
3 C. water
1 tsp. salt
1/3 C. butter
1/4 C. milk
1 tsp. garlic powder
Salt and pepper to taste
1/2 lb. chopped, cooked ham

In a large skillet or pot, place potatoes and water; sprinkle with 1 tsp. salt. Cover and cook potatoes over medium-high heat, stirring occasionally until potatoes are tender. Drain. Stir in butter, milk, garlic powder, salt, pepper, and ham.

You can use 8 slices bacon, cooked and crumbled, instead of the ham in this recipe.

Notes & Tips

Cook twice the beef, chicken, or ham for your dinner. Cooking time isn't much longer, and leftovers may be used for sandwiches and casseroles.

PEP
SALT
Simply Sandwiches

Quick Roast Beef Sandwiches

1 10 1/2-oz. can French onion soup
1 T. Worcestershire sauce
12 thin slices deli roast beef
6 soft hoagie buns
6 slices deli provolone cheese
Pickled banana pepper rings, drained

In a medium saucepan, combine soup and Worcestershire; bring to a boil. Add beef and heat through. Split buns and place on a baking sheet. Using a slotted spoon, place meat mixture on bun bottoms. Top with cheese slices. Broil 4–5 inches from heat about 1 minute or until cheese is melted and bubbly. Place banana peppers and top bun over cheese.

Above all else, children need to know and feel they are loved, wanted, and appreciated.

Ezra Taft Benson

Hot French Dip Sandwiches

2 T. butter
1 T. all-purpose flour
2 cans beef consomme or beef broth
2 green onions, chopped (opt.)
2 lbs. deli-sliced roast beef
6 kaiser or hard rolls, split

In a large skillet over medium heat, melt butter. Stir flour into butter until well blended. Whisk in consomme or broth in a slow stream. Stir in green onions. Bring sauce to a low boil, stirring continually. Reduce heat and simmer over low heat until ready to serve. Using a pair of kitchen tongs, dip meat into au jus sauce and pile into rolls.

Divide remaining au jus among individual cups or bowls and serve with sandwiches.

Philly Beef and Cheese Melts

3-lb. boneless beef chuck pot roast
1 onion, chopped
1/4 C. Worcestershire sauce
1 T. beef bouillon granules
2 cloves garlic, minced
2 tsp. Italian seasoning
8 hoagie buns or kaiser rolls
8 slices provolone cheese
1/2 C. pickled jalapeño peppers, sliced (opt.)

In a slow-cooker, combine meat, onion, Worcestershire sauce, bouillon granules, garlic, and Italian seasoning. Cover and cook on low for 8–9 hours or on high 4–5 hours. Using two forks, shred meat. Preheat oven broiler. Open buns and place on a baking sheet. Using a slotted spoon, place meat mixture on bun bottoms. Top with cheese. Broil 4–5 inches from heat about 1 minute or until cheese is melted and bubbly. Spread jalapeño peppers over melted cheese.

Barbecue Beef Sandwiches

1 3-lb. beef brisket or chuck pot roast
1 C. ginger ale or lemon-lime soda
2 T. Worcestershire sauce
1 T. chili powder
3 C. bottled barbecue sauce
1 onion, thinly sliced (opt.)
8 kaiser rolls or hamburger buns, split

Place meat in a 4-quart slow-cooker. Add soda, Worcestershire sauce, and chili powder. Cover and cook on low for 8–9 hours or high for 4–5 hours. Using two forks, shred meat. Stir in barbecue sauce. Cover and cook on high for 10–15 minutes or until heated through. Spoon into split kaiser rolls or hamburger buns. If desired, serve with sliced onions. Makes 12 to 16 sandwiches.

May also be served with dill pickles.

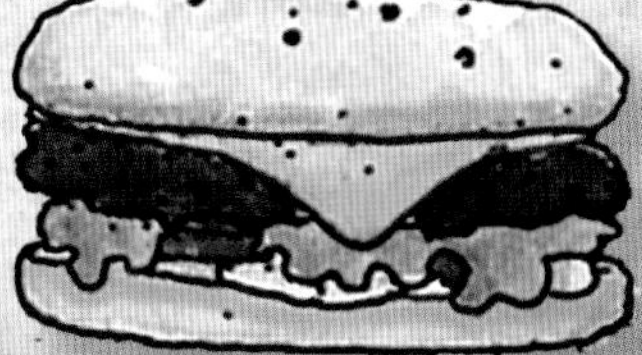

Original Pulled Pork Sandwiches

3- to 4-lb. boneless pork roast
1/2 tsp. each salt and pepper
1 C. brown sugar
1/2 env. taco seasoning
1 12-oz. can lemon-lime soda
1 16-oz. bottle barbecue sauce
Kaiser rolls or hamburger buns

Place meat in a 4-quart slow-cooker. Sprinkle salt and pepper, brown sugar, and taco seasoning over pork roast. Pour soda around sides of pork roast. Cover and cook on low for 8–9 hours or high for 4–5 hours. Using two forks to pull, shred meat. Stir in barbecue sauce. Cover and cook on high for 10–15 minutes or until heated through. Spoon into split kaiser rolls or hamburger buns.

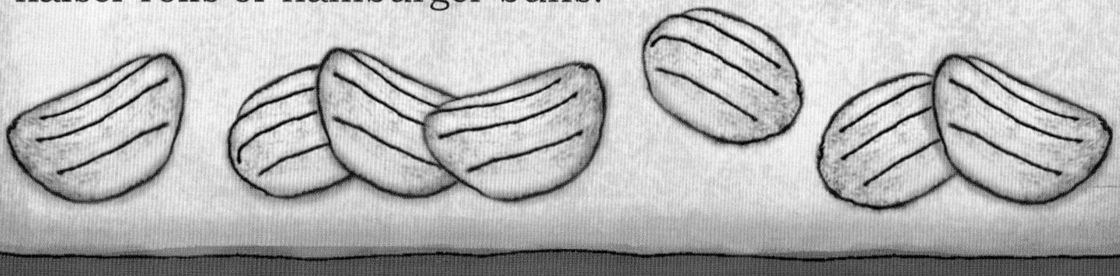

Italian Sausage Sandwiches

6–8 links hot or mild Italian sausage
1 medium red bell pepper, thinly sliced
1 medium green bell pepper, thinly sliced
1 medium onion, thinly sliced
2 T. olive oil or vegetable oil
1/4 C. butter, softened (opt.)
2 tsp. garlic salt (opt.)
6–8 hot dog buns
1 C. mozzarella cheese

Boil sausage links 8–10 minutes or until sausages are done. Meanwhile, sauté peppers and onions in oil until tender and onions begin to turn golden brown. In a separate bowl, combine butter and garlic salt. Preheat broiler. Open buns and place on a baking sheet. Spread garlic butter over buns. Place sausage links in buns and sprinkle with mozzarella cheese. Broil open-faced for 1–2 minutes. Place pepper-onion mixture over sausages and serve hot.

Quick Meatball Subs

1 tsp. vegetable oil
1 16-oz. bag frozen cooked Italian-style meatballs (1- to 1 1/2-inch)
1 16-oz. jar tomato pasta sauce
6–8 hoagie buns, split and toasted
1 C. shredded mozzarella cheese

In a medium skillet, heat oil over medium-high heat until hot. Add meatballs and cook 2–3 minutes, stirring frequently, until meatballs are heated through. Add pasta sauce and continue cooking, stirring occasionally, until thoroughly heated. Spoon meatballs and sauce into each hoagie bun. Sprinkle with cheese.

If desired, you can make your own meatballs. Follow recipe on page 81 for Meatloaf Muffins but shape meat into 1-inch balls. Cook meatballs in hot oil over medium-high heat 5–6 minutes or until meatballs are cooked through. Continue as directed in above recipe.

Sloppy Joes

2 lb. ground beef
1/2 env. sloppy joe seasoning mix
1 stalk celery, finely diced
1 onion, finely diced
1 carrot, peeled and shredded
2 15-oz. cans crushed tomatoes
1/2 C. tomato ketchup
2 T. yellow mustard
1/4 C. white sugar
8–12 hamburger buns

In a large skillet or stock pot, cook ground beef with salt, pepper, and garlic powder to taste. Drain fat. Stir in remaining ingredients. Cover and simmer over medium-low heat, stirring often, 15–20 minutes or until vegetables are tender. Serve on hamburger buns.

enjoy the little things in life; one day you will look back and see they were the big things.

Chicken Roll-Ups

2 8-oz. pkgs. cream cheese
1 1/2 C. chopped, cooked chicken

2 8-count cans refrigerated crescent rolls
***1 can cream of chicken soup**
***1/2 soup can of milk**

Soften cream cheese in microwave. Combine chicken and cream cheese. Roll out crescent rolls. Spread a large spoonful of chicken mixture in center of each roll. Roll up crescents and pinch edges to seal. Place rolls on ungreased baking sheet. Bake at 350 for 20–25 minutes or until rolls are golden.

Garlic Chicken Roll-Ups: In a small bowl, combine 1/2 C. bread crumbs, 1 T. Parmesan cheese, and 1/2 tsp. garlic salt. Brush rolls with melted butter and roll in bread crumb mixture. Place rolls on ungreased baking sheet. Bake at 350 for 20–25 minutes or until rolls are golden.

*If desired, in a small saucepan combine cream of chicken soup and milk. Heat through. Serve over chicken roll-ups.

Pigs in a Blanket

8 hot dogs
1 8–count can refrigerated crescent rolls

Separate dough into triangles. Wrap one dough triangle around each hot dog. Place on ungreased baking sheet. Bake at 375 for 12–15 minutes or until golden brown.

Cheesy Pigs in a Blanket: Cut 4 slices American cheddar cheese into quarters. Slit hot dogs to within 1/2 inch of each end; insert 2 quarters of cheese into slit of each hot dog. Repeat with remaining hot dogs. Follow directions above for wrapping in rolls. Place on ungreased baking sheet cheese side up. Bake as directed above.

Mini Pigs in a Blanket: Cut hot dogs in half; cut each half lengthwise (making 32 mini hot dogs). Unroll dough but leave 2 triangles of crescent rolls intact. Pinch seam together and cut lengthwise into 4 strips and then once crosswise to make 8 strips. Repeat until you have 32 dough strips. Roll each strip around one mini hot dog. Bake as directed above.

Ham and Cheese Hot Pockets

6 slices of ham, chopped
1 C. shredded cheddar cheese
2 8–count cans refrigerated crescent rolls

In a small bowl, combine chopped ham and cheese. Press crescent rolls to flatten. Place ham and cheese mixture at center of 1/2 of the roll. Place a second roll on top of ham and cheese mixture. Pull edges of bottom roll up over top roll; pinch dough together to seal edges. Place on greased baking sheet. Repeat with remaining rolls. Bake at 375 for 15–20 minutes or until golden brown.

Broccoli and Cheese Hot Pockets: Add 1 C. frozen broccoli florets, thawed and chopped, to the ham and cheese mixture. Continue as directed.

A happy family is but an earlier heaven

John Bowring

Pizza Pockets

2 8–count cans refrigerated crescent rolls
1 26-oz. jar tomato pasta sauce
1 3-oz. pkg. pepperoni slices, chopped
1 C. shredded mozzarella cheese

Press crescent rolls to flatten. Spread 1–2 T. tomato pasta sauce at center of flattened roll. Sprinkle chopped pepperoni and shredded mozzarella cheese over sauce. Pull edges of bottom roll up over top roll; pinch rolls together at edges to seal. Place on greased baking sheet. Repeat with remaining rolls. Bake at 375 for 15–20 minutes or until golden brown.

If desired, you can add mushrooms, peppers, olives, onions, or other pizza ingredients to this recipe.

Hawaiian Delight Pizza Pockets: Replace chopped pepperoni with chopped ham or Canadian bacon and pineapple tidbits. Continue as directed.

Personal Pizzas

2 8–count cans refrigerated crescent rolls
1 26-oz. jar tomato pasta sauce
1 3-oz. pkg. pepperoni slices, chopped
1 C. shredded mozzarella cheese

Press 2 crescent rolls together to make a ball; flatten ball into a circle. Place flattened circles 1 inch apart on greased baking sheet. Spread tomato pasta sauce to within 1/2 inch of edges. Sprinkle shredded mozzarella cheese and pepperoni slices over sauce. Bake at 425 for 10–15 minutes or until golden brown on edges. If desired, add mushrooms, peppers, olives, onions, or other toppings.

Cheesy Bread–Bites: Press rolls into 1-inch balls. Combine 1/4 C. melted butter with 1 tsp. garlic salt. Dip rolls in garlic butter; roll in dry Parmesan cheese. Bake as directed above.

French Bread Pizza

1 loaf French bread, unsliced
1 26-oz. jar tomato pasta sauce
1 1/2 C. shredded cheddar cheese
1 lb. ground beef, cooked and drained
1 6.5-oz. can ripe olives, drained and sliced

Slice French bread in half lengthwise. Place top and bottom pieces open-faced on ungreased baking sheet. Broil 1–2 minutes or until lightly toasted. Remove from oven. Spread tomato pasta sauce over bread. Sprinkle with cheese, ground beef, and olives. Return to oven. Bake at 450 for 8–10 minutes or until cheese is melted and bubbly.

If desired, you can substitute mozzarella cheese for the cheddar cheese and pepperoni for the ground beef. Other toppings may also be added as desired.

Pizza Burgers: Use hamburger buns instead of French bread. Follow directions above for toasting buns. Continue as directed.

Creamy Tuna Salad Sandwiches

12 slices white or wheat sandwich bread
2 5–oz. cans water-pack tuna, drained
1/2 C. mayonnaise or salad dressing
1/2 C. chopped iceberg lettuce
1 tomato, finely diced
Salt and pepper to taste

In a small bowl, combine tuna, mayonnaise or salad dressing, lettuce, tomato, salt, and pepper. If desired, spread butter or mayonnaise on bread slices.
Spread tuna salad over half of the slices.
Top with remaining bread slices.

Chopped dill pickles, celery, and/or onions may be added to this recipe. If desired, add cheese slices to these sandwiches.

Hot Tuna Melts

12 slices white or wheat sandwich bread
2 5–oz. cans water-pack tuna, drained
1/2 C. mayonnaise or salad dressing
Salt and pepper to taste
6 slices Swiss or mozzarella cheese

Lightly toast 6 slices of bread. In a small bowl, combine tuna, mayonnaise, salt, and pepper. Spread tuna mixture on the toasted bread slices. Place on an ungreased baking sheet. Place cheese slices on tuna. Broil on high 1–2 minutes until cheese is melted and bubbly. Toast remaining 6 slices of bread and place on melted cheese.

REJOICE WITH YOUR *family* IN THE BEAUTIFUL LAND OF LIFE

ALBERT EINSTEIN

Boiled Egg Salad Sandwiches

6 large eggs
6 T. Miracle Whip salad dressing
1 tsp. yellow mustard
1/4 tsp. salt
1/8 tsp. paprika
12 slices white or wheat sandwich bread

In a small saucepan, hard-boil eggs by covering with cool water. Sprinkle with salt (to aid in peeling the eggs). Bring to a boil over medium-high heat. Turn off heat and allow eggs to sit in hot water 6 minutes. Run eggs under cold water. Peel and rinse eggs; pat dry. In a small mixing bowl, mash eggs with a fork. Stir in salad dressing, mustard, salt, and paprika. Spread on half of the bread slices. Top with remaining bread slices.

Serve with lettuce leaves.

Chopped Bologna Sandwiches

4 eggs
8 slices bologna or 2 5-oz. cans potted meat
1 C. Miracle Whip salad dressing
1/2 C. sweet pickle relish
12 slices white or wheat sandwich bread

Follow directions on opposite page for hard-boiling eggs. Grind the bologna and eggs in a meat grinder with a medium blade or chop bologna and eggs; combine in a medium bowl. Stir in salad dressing and sweet pickle relish. Spread on half of the bread slices. Top with remaining bread slices.

Ham may be substituted for the bologna in this recipe.

We all desire to improve our performance as parents. No task is more common, yet none is more important.

Joseph F. Smith

Chicken Salad Croissants

6–8 large croissant rolls
1/2 C. mayonnaise
1/2 C. sour cream
1/2 tsp. each salt and pepper
1 1/2 C. shredded chicken breast meat
3/4 C. chopped celery
1 C. red grapes, halved
1/4 C. finely diced onion
1/4 C. sweet pickle relish (opt.)

Slice croissant rolls (cut in half if desired); set aside. In a medium bowl, mix mayonnaise, sour cream, salt, and pepper until well blended. Stir in shredded chicken, chopped celery, grapes, onion, and relish. Fill croissants. Eat immediately.

You may use dinner rolls instead of croissants in this recipe. This recipe fills 1–2 dozen dinner rolls.

Old-Fashioned Turkey Salad Rolls

This is a great recipe for using leftover turkey meat!

2 C. chopped, cooked turkey (white or dark meat)
1/2 C. mayonnaise or salad dressing
1/2 C. chopped sweet pickles
12 dinner rolls

In a small bowl, combine turkey, mayonnaise, and sweet pickles. Slice rolls and fill with turkey salad.

Chicken Salad Rolls: Follow above recipe for turkey salad but replace turkey with 3 C. chopped, cooked chicken. Add 1/2 C. chopped lettuce, 1/2 C. finely diced onion, and 1/2 C. chopped tomatoes. Continue as directed.

Notes & Tips

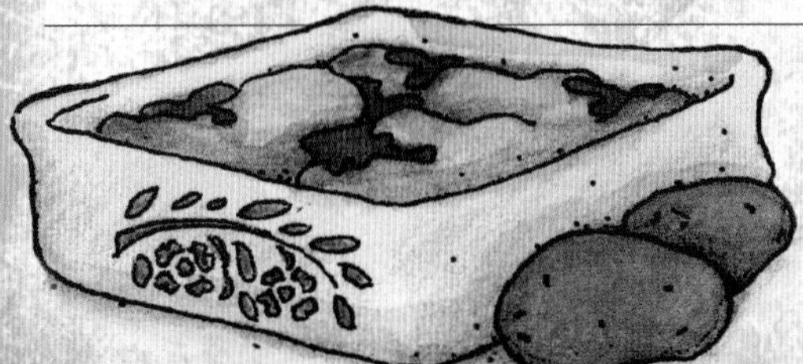

Have leftover night. Everyone chooses what he or she wants from the the fridge and heats it in the microwave.

Easy Desserts

Hot Fudge Molten Chocolate Cake

1/2 C. butter, melted
4 squares unsweetened chocolate
3/4 C. granulated sugar
2 eggs + 2 egg yolks, well beaten
3/4 C. flour

In a mixing bowl, combine the melted butter and chocolate. Stir in sugar. Fold in beaten eggs and flour until well blended. Thoroughly coat 6 custard cups with nonstick cooking spray and place them on a baking sheet. Divide batter among cups. Bake at 350 for 12–13 minutes or until cakes are no longer jiggly. Allow to cool 3–5 minutes. Invert custard cups onto serving plates. Serve with vanilla ice cream.

You may replace the unsweetened chocolate squares with 1/2 C. unsweetened cocoa powder.

No-Bake Peanut Butter Bars

1 C. butter, melted
2 C. graham cracker crumbs
2 C. powdered sugar
1 C. peanut butter
1 1/2 C. semisweet chocolate chips
4 T. peanut butter

Combine butter, graham cracker crumbs, powdered sugar, and 1 C. peanut butter until well blended. Press evenly in an ungreased 9x13 baking pan. Melt chocolate chips and peanut butter, stirring occasionally until smooth. Spread over peanut butter crust. Refrigerate until chocolate cools.

No-Bake Chocolate Cookies: In a heavy saucepan, bring to a boil 1/2 C. butter, 2 C. sugar, 4 T. cocoa, and 1 T. milk. Boil for 1 minute; add 1 C. peanut butter, 1 T. vanilla, and 3 C. oatmeal. Drop mixture by teaspoonfuls onto a greased baking sheet or waxed paper; cool until hardened.

No-Bake Chocolate Cream Cake

2 3.5-oz. boxes instant chocolate pudding mix
3 C. milk
18 full graham cracker squares
1 12-oz. container whipped topping, thawed
Chocolate syrup

In a medium bowl, beat pudding mix and milk until well blended. In a 9x13 baking dish, make 3 layers each of 6 graham crackers, 1/3 of the pudding, and 1/3 of the whipped topping. Drizzle with chocolate syrup. Refrigerate 30 minutes.

No-Bake Banana Cream Cake: Follow above recipe, but replace chocolate pudding mix with vanilla pudding mix. Peel and slice 3 bananas. Arrange sliced bananas on top of each layer of graham crackers. Omit chocolate syrup.

No-Bake Coconut Cream Cake: Replace sliced bananas in the Banana Cream Cake recipe with flaked coconut. Sprinkle 1/2 C. coconut evenly over each layer of pudding.

No-Bake Cheesecake

1 3-oz. box lemon gelatin mix
1 C. boiling water
1 8-oz. pkg. cream cheese, softened
1 9-in. graham cracker pie crust
Half of a 12-oz. container whipped topping
1 22-oz. can fruit pie filling (opt.)

Dissolve gelatin in boiling water. Place cream cheese in blender. Pour dissolved gelatin over cream cheese. Blend until smooth. Pour mixture into graham cracker crust. Stir in thawed whipped topping until well blended. Refrigerate until set (about 1 hour). If desired, spoon pie filling on top.

Chocolate Cheesecake

Substitute 1 6-oz. pkg. cheesecake-flavor instant pudding mix for the lemon gelatin and 2 C. milk for the boiling water. Replace pie filling with chocolate syrup. Drizzle syrup over cream cheese mixture. Drag a knife through chocolate to create marbled topping. Chill to set (15–20 minutes).

Ice Cream Cake

12 ice cream sandwiches
1 carton ice cream (any flavor)
Whipped topping
Ice cream syrup (any flavor)
1 giant candy bar (any flavor), broken up

Remove wrappers from ice cream sandwiches. Place 6 sandwiches on bottom of 9x13 baking pan. Completely open carton of ice cream. Cut ice cream into 1/2-inch slices and place over sandwiches until they are completely covered. Spread ice cream until fairly even. Place a second layer of sandwiches over the layer of ice cream. Spread whipped topping over sandwiches. Freeze until ready to serve. Before serving, drizzle with ice cream syrup and sprinkle with candy bar pieces.

To be sure your life will be full and abundant, you must plan your life.

Spencer W. Kimball

Easy Pudding Puffs

1 C. all-purpose flour
1/2 tsp. salt
6 eggs
1 C. milk
Pudding mix (any flavor)
Whipped topping or powdered sugar (opt.)

Sift flour and salt. Whisk eggs and milk into flour mixture until well blended. Generously butter a cupcake pan. Fill cups 1/3 to 1/2 full. Bake at 450 for 15 minutes or until edges are golden brown. Pierce sides with a sharp knife to allow steam to escape. Cut puffs in half. Fill with pudding and whipped topping. Replace tops. Top with whipped topping or sprinkle with powdered sugar.

Strawberry Puffs: Substitute strawberry topping for pudding—combine 1 C. sliced strawberries with 3 T. sugar; stir to dissolve sugar.

Fancy Fruit Trifle

1 3.4-oz. box instant vanilla pudding mix
1 C. milk
1 12-oz. container whipped topping, thawed
1 8-oz. container sour cream
1 9-in. angel food cake
1 15-oz. can crushed pineapple
3 bananas, peeled and sliced
3 kiwi fruit, peeled and sliced
1 pint fresh strawberries, sliced

In a medium bowl, beat pudding mix and milk until well blended. Fold in whipped topping and sour cream. Cut cake into thirds horizontally. Drain pineapple; reserve liquid. Soak sliced bananas in reserved liquid.

In a large trifle dish or glass serving bowl, line edges with kiwi and strawberry slices, reserving some for garnish. Make 3 layers of cake, bananas and pineapple, and pudding mixture. Garnish with remaining kiwi and strawberry slices.

Pretzel Raspberry Jell-O Dessert

2 1/2 C. coarsely crumbled pretzels
3/4 C. butter, melted
1 T. + 1/2 C. sugar
1 8-oz. pkg. cream cheese
1 tsp. vanilla
1 12-oz. pkg. frozen whipped topping
3 3-oz. pkg. raspberry Jell-O
1 C. boiling water
2 C. ice cubes
3 10-oz. boxes frozen raspberries

Mix pretzels, butter, and 1 T. sugar; press into a 9x13 ungreased baking dish. Bake at 400 for 8 minutes; cool. Meanwhile, beat cream cheese, 1/2 C. sugar, and vanilla until smooth. Stir in whipped topping. Spread cream cheese mixture over cooled pretzel mixture. Dissolve Jell-O in boiling water. Stir in ice cubes and frozen raspberries. Pour over cream cheese mixture and refrigerate 1 hour or until set.

Fruity Ice Cream

1 C. half-and-half
1/4 C. sugar
1 tsp. vanilla
1–2 C. frozen fruit (any variety)

In a blender, combine half-and-half, sugar, and vanilla. Blend on high, dropping in a few pieces frozen fruit at a time, until thick and creamy. Recipe makes about 2 1/2 C. ice cream. (Repeat recipe to make more!)

Chocolate Banana Ice Cream: Reduce sugar to 3 T. Replace vanilla with 2–3 T. chocolate syrup. Use peeled frozen bananas for fruit. Blend as directed.

Low-Fat Fruity Ice Cream: Replace half-and-half with 1 C. milk.

Fruit and Yogurt Parfaits

1 32-oz. container vanilla yogurt
4 T. instant vanilla pudding powder
4 C. frozen berries (strawberries, raspberries blueberries, blackberries, etc.)
1/4 C. granulated sugar
Oat and honey granola bars, broken up

Mix yogurt with pudding powder. Refrigerate until ready to serve. Place frozen berries in a medium mixing bowl; if necessary, cut into smaller chunks. Sprinkle berries with sugar; stir until dissolved. Layer yogurt, fruit, and granola in individual cups.

Fruity Yogurt Pops: Layer yogurt (any flavor) and fresh fruit in 3-oz. paper cups. Cover each cup with plastic wrap. Poke sticks through plastic wrap to bottom of cup. Freeze until ready to serve. Tear paper from yogurt pops before serving.

Easy Blueberry Peach Cobbler

4 C. peeled and sliced peaches
1/2 C. maple syrup
2 boxes Jiffy Blueberry Muffin mix
1/2 C. milk

Spread peaches in a 9x13 baking dish. Pour maple syrup over peaches. Combine muffin mix and milk; drop by spoonfuls on top of peaches. Bake at 350 for 30 minutes. Serve with ice cream or whipped topping.

Apple Cinnamon Peach Cobbler: Use Jiffy brand Apple Cinnamon Muffin mix instead of the Blueberry Muffin mix.

Quick Peach Cobbler: Substitute 1 quart bottle (or 29-oz. can) sliced peaches (drained) for the fresh peaches in this recipe. Omit the maple syrup.

Dessert Waffles

1/2 C. butter, melted
1 egg + 1 egg white, well beaten
1 C. sugar
1 C. milk
1 tsp. vanilla
1 C. flour
Pinch salt
1/2 tsp. baking powder

Whisk the melted butter and whole egg until well blended. Using a hand mixer, beat egg white until peaks form. Fold into egg mixture. Stir in sugar, milk, and vanilla. Sift flour, salt, and baking powder. Stir into egg mixture. Pour onto heated waffle iron. Cook until golden brown. Top with fruit topping, ice cream, or whipped topping.

Waffle Ice Cream Sandwiches: Slice ice cream (any flavor) to 1/2- to 3/4-inch thickness. Place ice cream slices between 2 dessert waffles. Press together to make an ice cream sandwich.

Instant Waffles: Prepare a cake mix (any flavor) according to package directions. Cook in waffle maker until golden.

Microwave Bundt Chocolate Cake

1 16-oz. container chocolate frosting
1 15.25-oz. chocolate cake mix

Frost sides of a microwave-safe *bundt pan with chocolate frosting. Prepare cake mix according to package directions. Pour into prepared bundt pan. Cook at 70 percent power 11 minutes, then full power 1 minute. Let stand 15–20 minutes.

** If you do not have a microwave-safe bundt pan, you can use an 8- to 9-inch microwave-safe bowl. Place a microwave-safe glass upside down in the center of the bowl. Frost sides of bowl and glass. Continue as directed above.*

German Chocolate Bundt Cake

Follow above directions, using coconut pecan frosting and German chocolate cake mix.

Instant Brownies

1/4 C. butter
2 T. cocoa powder
1/2 C. sugar
1 egg
1/2 tsp. vanilla
1/2 C. all-purpose flour
1/4 tsp. baking powder
Dash of salt

Melt butter in an 8x8 microwave-safe dish. Stir in cocoa and sugar until well blended. Fold in egg and vanilla. Sift flour, baking powder, and salt; fold into cocoa mixture. Cook on high for 3 minutes. Let stand 5 minutes.

Personal Mug Cake

In a large bowl, mix 1 C. flour, 1 C. sugar, 1/2 C. cocoa, 2 eggs, 3/4 C. milk, 3/4 C. vegetable oil, 1/2 tsp. vanilla, and a dash salt. Spray 4 mugs with nonstick cooking spray. Microwave each cake individually on high for 2 minutes.

INDEX

D

E

F

G

H